Virtual

Migration

Virtual
Migration

The Programming of Globalization

A. ANEESH

DUKE UNIVERSITY PRESS | DURHAM AND LONDON | 2006

© 2006 Duke University Press

All rights reserved

Printed in the United States of America on acid-free paper ∞

Designed by Heather Hensley

Typeset in Adobe Garamond by Tseng Information Systems, Inc.

Library of Congress Cataloging-in-Publication Data appear
on the last printed page of this book.

For mummy and babuji

Contents

Acknowledgments

As I look back, a number of conversations, writings, faces, and smiles come into view. Perhaps "gratitude," not acknowledgment, is the word. A deep sense of gratitude overwhelms my memory of the period when this book was conceived, researched, and written. Individualizing frames of authorship aside, the book is an extraordinary kind of debt free from a demand for any return. Borrowed ideas, freely available frames of analysis, active mentoring, and support from many people and institutions made possible the work, which fits in more with the notion of "putting together" than with the romantic notion of authorship. While the author unavoidably disappears behind his writing, which frees itself from the author through the reader's assigned meanings, I do take responsibility for any failure in creating a fresh opening into the subject of globalization. My first expression of gratitude goes to József Böröcz, who has been to me a combination of diverse categories: advisor, colleague, and friend. Without his encouragement this work would not have been completed. Special thanks are due to Lee Clarke and Eviatar Zerubavel, who advised and supported me through the entire process of conception, research, and writing. I must also thank Saskia Sassen not only for her intellectual presence in my work but also for her support and mentoring during all these years. They all helped in shaping an academic career and giving it direction.

I am deeply indebted to the software companies that allowed me to visit their premises as well as all the executives and programmers who agreed to have conversations with me.

A few institutions contributed greatly toward the completion of this work. First, I thank the Sociology Department and all the associated people at Rutgers University, which remained a ground for learning and professional socialization for many years. The Population Council and the International Migration Program of the Social Science Research Council, with their generous field research fellowships, were central to the empirical research that informs this book. The Social Science Research Council's Program on Information Technology, International Cooperation and Global Security facilitated an intense period of writing at the University of California, Berkeley, in 2001. I thank Monica Biradavolu, a summer fellow at Berkeley, whose intellectual companionship was crucial in that phase of writing.

This book contains, even though in a highly dispersed and possibly un-recognizable form, some of my earlier ideas and writings that have appeared in journals and edited books. I thank the editors and publishers for giving early recognition to those writings. In particular, I express gratitude to the editors and publishers of *Theory and Society* for publishing an article on skill saturation (2001); Wayne Cornelius, Thomas Espenshade, Idean Salehyan, and the Center for Comparative Immigration Studies, University of California, San Diego, for reviewing, editing, and publishing an article in the book *The International Migration of the Highly Skilled: Demand, Supply, and Development Consequences* (2001); and Colin Wayne Leach, Dona Gabaccia, and Routledge for reviewing, editing, and publishing an article for *Immigrant Life in the United States: Multi-disciplinary Perspectives* (2003). I acknowledge with appreciation the feedback provided by the audiences at professional meetings—the American Sociological Association, the American Anthropological Association, the Society for Social Studies of Science, and the International Summer Academy on Technology Studies (Austria)—as the work was being written. I am also thankful to the Berkeley Center for Globalization and Information Technology at the University of California, Berkeley; the Center for Science, Technology and Society at Santa Clara University; the Institute for the Future in Menlo Park; International Studies in Planning at Cornell University; and the Globalization Forum at Diablo Valley College, California, for inviting me to deliver lectures where I could articulate the ideas developed in this book.

I thank my friends, colleagues, and mentors Akhil Gupta, Jim Ferguson, Paula Findlen, Sarah Jain, Liisa Malkki, Robert McGinn, and Fred Turner, whose support during my stint at Stanford University and beyond was invaluable. And let me not forget my friends from Rutgers: Alena Alamgir, Rachel Askew, Wayne Brekhus, Rebecca Kissane, Julie McLaughlin, Rick Phillips, and Anna Da Silva, whose intellectual, if often slightly inebriated, company at a local bar in New Brunswick offered both stimulation and respite during the initial, conceptual phase of research. Alexandru Balasescu, Marie Cieri, Mohan and Deepa Gupta, Eric Kaldor, and Monika Mehta have been not only academic but also close family friends during this period. I am particularly grateful to Sudarshan Rao and Jyotsna Rao, whose home was always open to me and whose support was always available.

I am grateful to my family members in Seattle for their continuous support. I can only acknowledge, never repay, my debt to Paul Bornstein, who provided me with office space in Seattle, among many other gifts, for two consecutive summers of writing and revisions. During these periods I stayed with Gloria Bornstein and Yasuo Mori, who kept their home and hearts open to a degree quite rare in everyday life today.

I want to thank the editorial team of Duke University Press, particularly Ken Wissoker, Courtney Berger, and Raphael Allen, for taking active interest in this work, as well as the promotion and production team at Duke, including Katie Courtland, Heather Hensley, Michael McCullough, Lee Willoughby-Harris, and Emily Young. I also want to thank my copy-editor, Fred Kameny, under whose watchful eyes the book attained order and clarity.

I offer gratitude to my family members in India for being there while I was performing a task quite worthless to them. My thanks to all the friends in India must remain unstated, as verbal thanking in India is at once too much and too little. Too much because it threatens to turn informal relationships into formal ones, too little because open acknowledgments belittle the debt and relieve the debtor too quickly. And finally the person whose love I could take for granted was Erica Bornstein. She was not only the first to read, comment, and critique all my writing; she was, and forever is, the unwavering ground of my existence.

CHAPTER I

Of Code and Capital

A silent transformation in the global organization of work is upon us. With high-speed data-communication links, workers based in one part of the world are increasingly able to work at locations far beyond their immediate horizon. Other stories of globalization and migration have commonly centered around the body, narrating how laboring bodies move from the developing to developed nations (see for example MacPhee and Hassan 1990; Zlotnick 1998), and how the integration of transnational labor—both documented and undocumented—takes place and struggles along national borders. Indeed, over the years the border has only grown in significance. In the decade after 1993 the U.S. Border Patrol doubled in size and tripled its budget; for migrants as well, the border has become costlier, in terms of increased *coyote*[1] fees and also in lives—between 1994 and 2001 the bodies of more than 2,700 failed migrants[2] were regularly recovered on both sides of the border between the United States and Mexico (Cornelius 2001). The border has not lost its significance, of course. But there is a development in labor migration that negotiates national borders differently. This book contrasts the account of embodied migration with the fast-growing but little researched virtual migration that does not require workers to move in physical space.

This story unfurls an emerging paradigm of transnational labor that allows workers in India to connect to corporations and consumers in the United States with high-speed satellite and cable links, performing through globally accessible data servers a range of work activities. One type of work, the staffing of call centers, has come under the focus of the news media. As inquiries from Americans who watch infomercials are routed to India, a teleworker in New Delhi may be selling them badly needed tummy crunchers, diet pills, orthopedic insoles, or even a fitness machine. Other work activities do not depend on the telephone: software research and development, engineering and design, animation, geographic information systems, processing of insurance claims, accounting, data entry, transcription, translation, and customer services such as technical support. Features of this labor integration may include a continuous monitoring of work by the client in the United States, who can perform quality checks and communicate with Indian workers as if they were on site. Since the United States and India have an average time-zone difference of twelve hours, the client may enjoy, for a number of tasks, virtually round-the-clock office hours: when America closes its offices, India gets ready to start its day. Thus paradoxically, the new space of transnational labor has reversed its relationship with the worker's body. Rather than move the body across enormous distances, new mechanisms allow it to stay put while moving vast quantities of data at the speed of light.

In an increasingly integrated global economy, therefore, a different kind of labor migration is taking place. I call it *virtual migration*. Although emerging online labor is part of the common trend in contemporary capitalism to tap globally dispersed labor in a more flexible manner, it has three distinctive features. First, online labor has limited direct, physical, face-to-face contact with corporations in the United States. Second, one could argue that online work is hardly transnational in character, as it takes place within national boundaries, and in many instances in direct response to immigration restrictions. Thus workers in India, while indirectly working for American corporations through subcontracting firms, still retain a single, unambiguous national identity. Unlike immigrants who physically work in the United States, they do not go through the agony of visa requirements, alien status, cultural opposition, and "nativist reaction" (Cornelius, Martin, and Hollifield 1994). Third, workers based in India may (or may not) be governed by local practices, including labor and tax laws. Yet just like traditional immigrant workers, they do cross national boundaries and directly occupy some employment space in sectors of the American economy. In short, they migrate without migration, which is why we call the phenomenon virtual migration.

The concept of virtual migration underscores that a programmer sitting in India and working for a local firm can directly provide services in the United States, that a call center employee in Delhi—who sits in front of a computer screen wearing a headset—may sell a miniature rotisserie to a Californian. Many software development strategies rely on transnational software platforms that integrate groups sitting across the globe. Such invisible and disembodied processes of labor supply add a different dimension to our conventional understanding of labor migration.

I seek to free the discussion of labor mobility from the confines of the body, and to place the flows of labor at the level of global capital flows. This approach enables us to see certain social aspects of the transnational integration of labor that remain invisible in the economistic language of outsourcing and subcontracting. There are also semantic differences between outsourcing, offshoring, and virtual migration. Outsourcing is a relatively undifferentiated umbrella term, covering aspects of offshoring and virtual migration as well as the subcontracting of services and manufacturing within the country. Offshoring, on the other hand, surely happens off the shore or overseas, and it may include manufactured goods and components along with services. Virtual migration differs from outsourcing and offshoring in two respects: first, it does not include the transfer of physical merchandise such as parts, components, or the whole product, as it literally implies virtual labor integration, not trade in merchandise. Second, it encompasses the noneconomic elements that always accompany any mode of migration (such as the sociocultural aspects of call centers).

To bring out the uniqueness of these online labor flows from India to the United States, I compare them to the corresponding physical practice of securing work visas for Indian programmers and bringing them to the United States to work on site—a practice called "body shopping."[3] While online programming implies migration of skills but not of bodies, body shopping implies migration of both bodies and skills. Discussing the software engineering projects undertaken online as well as those undertaken on site, I attempt a different perspective on prevailing immigration debates in the United States as it relates to high-tech workers by exploring the changing channels of labor supply. As the majority of labor in the United States is increasingly being converted into information work—especially in the service sector that occupies a large employment space in the economy—I try to link the issues of the online delivery of work across national borders with immigration as well as with questions of globalization and technology.

Recent years have witnessed a quantum jump in books on globalization; yet there is still no account, to my knowledge, of the transnational space where globalization gets enacted or, rather, programmed. Serious scholarship has been a little suspicious of "virtual" spaces. In the 1990s the term "virtual" perhaps set off too much inflated rhetoric: it has been used too readily and too insistently in the dreams and discourses of the global village. Indeed, the virtual has turned out to be not so "virtual" after all. A recent work (Pellow and Park 2002) deflates pretensions of the high-tech industry as heralding a "third wave," which would transport humanity from the polluted and heavy materiality of the industrial age to a clean, light, and virtual information age. Silicon Valley—a putative center of the virtual universe—is littered with "Superfund" sites—the primary targets of toxic waste cleanup efforts. The "clean industry" has been dumping so much sewage laced with heavy metals like nickel, cyanide, lead, and cadmium into the San Francisco Bay that oysters and shellfish have become unsafe for human consumption. Why do we need to reestablish, then, the ill-fated virtual? My discussion of the term is different. I do not discuss "virtual" as a metaphor to signify all that is clean, global, and free from material stain. I dare not use it even as an ideal type that imposes a constructed unity on the slippery empirical. Eschewing the double of ideal and empirical as well as the binary opposition of the virtual and the material, I justify its usage for several other reasons: if words acquire meaning through use (Wittgenstein 1972), then virtual is already part of a network of speech acts with serious meaning for its users—thus virtual communities are not a figment of our imagination but part of the changing social landscape (see Turner forthcoming; Wellman, Salaff, Dimitrova, Garton, Gulia, and Haythornthwaite 1996). It is counterproductive and somewhat hopeless to undo well-established speech patterns, or worse, deny their existence; it would be more useful perhaps to locate the conditions of their emergence, and examine their social effects. Second, in my analysis virtual practices are quite concrete, grounded in programming languages and code whose materiality, as readable and undeniable as the words on this page, does not need to be deduced from unverified premises or generalized from particular events. Virtual migration is a measurable flow of code, containing work performance and skilled acts. Finally, I also hope to uncover in the course of this discussion the whole range of changes that virtual migration accompanies in terms of corporate, labor, and social organization.

One of the questions to ask is how this transnational virtual space is constituted. What modes of power and governance make it possible for this space to become the *organizing* space of transnational labor? Programming languages—rather understudied components of transnational work—appear to be the key organizing structures behind this emerging space, which in itself is neither national nor global. Instead it is symptomatic of a new kind of power, what I call *algocracy*—rule of the algorithm, or rule of the code, which perhaps constitutes the key difference between the current and previous rounds of global integration. As programming languages increasingly form an ever-present horizon of diverse work ranging from controlling heavy machines to typing this document, it is no mere accident that *programming* and *coding* are intrinsic to the emerging transnational labor regime, which is ordered and integrated through different relations of power and governance. Even call centers that may at first sight seem free from programming do not predate developments in software, for they are dependent on data servers and computer screens to carry out their work. This is why they are usually housed in software firms, representing only one component of their business.

Focusing on offshore online work between India and the United States, I understand that work is globally organized around three kinds of integration: (1) spatial integration, or the decoupling of work performance and work site; (2) temporal integration, or the real-time unification of different time zones; and (3) algocratic integration, or the role of programming languages or code in connecting transnationally dispersed labor through data servers. The three integrations highlight vital features of globalization programs, imagining and implementing a different organization and networking of capital, labor, and corporations in the electronic space of programming languages.

One may raise an obvious question: Why should we think of virtual migration as a transformation and not as a mere extension of the earlier capitalist trajectory toward global expansion? Why the rhetoric of novelty? The answer lies in the framing of the questions themselves. As a theoretical frame, I do prefer the language of "transformation" and "difference" over that of "continuity" or "linear successions." While I respect, and even participate in, the historical paradigm of linking disparate events through causal mechanisms, I also wish to suspend at times the epistemological belief in how they all link to original forerunners in a linear trajectory. As all knowledge is produced within certain discourses and linguistic frameworks, to be able to say that there is a trans-historical constant in capitalism linking the nineteenth century with the twenty-first century, we must employ a certain paradigm of causal connection (profit orientation, accumulation), but only with an awareness that this is just one of the many possible ways of integrating the events. Even in as hard a science as physics, there is some acceptance of this heuristic nature of causal models. I will quote one of the most respected names in physics, Stephen Hawking (1988)—no social constructivist—to illustrate the point: "a theory is just a model of the universe, or a restricted part of it, and a set of rules that relate quantities in the model to observations that we make. It exists *only in our minds* [or in our texts and instruments] and *does not have any other reality* (whatever that might mean) . . . Any physical theory is always provisional, in the sense that it is only a hypothesis: you can never prove it. No matter how many times the results of experiments agree with some theory, you can never be sure that the next time the result will not contradict the theory" (emphasis added).

Of course Hawking does not mean that science is mere fiction or pure imagination. Perhaps he is suggesting that the ability to predict future events does not save a theory from being a mere heuristic device. Newton's theory of gravity still accurately predicts the motions of the moon, the sun, and the planets but it is no longer the dominant paradigm for causal explanations in physics. Einstein's theory of relativity changes the very understanding of gravity, which is no longer the force between two bodies but an effect of the fact that space-time is curved or "warped" around massive bodies such as the sun and the earth. The earth revolves around the sun not because there is a force called gravity; instead, it follows the closest thing to a straight path in a curved space, that is, a geodesic. The word "gravity" in itself is empty; it gains its specific meaning only after its insertion into a system of significa- tion (Newtonian or Einsteinian physics). Even though words such as "space," "time," and "gravity" remain in use, they mean something entirely different after what Kuhn (1962) called the *paradigm shift*, marking a complete trans- formation in causal explanations. If the "scientific fact" concerning "what causes the Earth to revolve around the Sun" can change so dramatically, one may be allowed some room in discussing such pitiably soft phenomena as capitalism and migration.

The language of "transformation" or "difference" also opens up avenues of inquiry that are, well, different from those offered by the language of con- tinuity. For example, I may say that this book in its physical form continues to be the same thing that it was yesterday, but Bertrand Russell (1948)—who, again, is not our regular social constructivist—might suggest otherwise. The book is only quasi-permanent, because a piece of matter should not be regarded as a single, persistent, substantial entity but as a string of events occurring at a slightly earlier or later time at some neighboring place.[4] Adding the notion of temporality to existence, Russell abandons the very idea of "substance" to open up a different way of looking at the so-called identity of a thing or person, quite like the Buddhist description of the world as a flame where change appears as continuity, and difference as identity. With this orientation, it is not change and difference but unity and identity that require explanation. This is more than to suggest that we cannot take for granted the continuity and identity of capitalism through history. This is also not to suggest that virtual migration is a practice marking a change away from capitalism, or just a shift within capitalism, for that matter. The idea is to suspend the belief—useful as it may seem—that virtual migration is part of an existing whole, or an integrated field of capitalism. The effort lies in seeing it as produced by different ensembles that join, connect, and branch off in unforeseen directions. Theoretically this stance, with its focus on irreducible plurality, guards against producing an image of a single destiny or a retrospective reconstruction of the past as a linear development with the advantage of hindsight. It allows for unforeseen connections, surprises, and undetermined future possibilities.

Virtual migration in particular results from the marriage of two systems of governance: capital and code. Both appeared to enjoy relatively independent trajectories until the advent of computers in the twentieth century. The history of programming code can be traced back—at least discursively—to the Enlightenment, to the times of monarchy, and to Leibniz's dream of a universal artificial mathematical language in which all knowledge, with all the rules and logical interrelationships among propositions, could be expressed. Modern capital and programming code thus signify two universalisms that tend to overdetermine different aspects of life. I discuss this further in chapters 5 and 6.

There are two themes concerning capital and code that will surface time and again throughout the book: the first is the danger of conflating the economic and the social where the social is often assimilated to the economic (since economic development is often the dominant social objective of governments, corporations, and even individuals). Yet we know that what is economically good may not always be socially good. If two-fifths of all employed Americans work mostly at odd hours—in the evening, at night, on a rotating shift, or during the weekend, that does keep a fast-paced and seamlessly integrated 24/7 economy humming, yet it also indicates a simultaneous surrender of the social to the economic, colonizing the family and social lives of all involved (Presser 2003). If the Gross Domestic Product (GDP) grows, for instance, because of the excessive construction of prisons or the sale of antidepressants and other medications, it is hard to say that such developments are necessarily wonderful in social terms. The second concern, relating to code, is the increasing tendency to program certain outcomes in advance, reducing the domain of social negotiability. For example, code can replace many components of law by programming copyright protections into software and hardware systems (Lessig 1999), thus taking them out of the realm of negotiation, a central component of philosophical justifications for democracy.

The dominance of *programming*, *code*, and *information* in everyday life also suggests a larger transformation in the way disciplines, from cybernetics to psychology (Edwards 1996), think about the world and produce knowledge. Discourses of radically different disciplines such as biology and computer science increasingly organize around the language of code and communication. Under this discursive formation or epistemic shift, life itself is rendered into a language, for example the language of genetic code. The biological discourse constructs genetic ensembles, including humans, as systems of *information processing*, as programmed processes whose code, once rendered legible, allows the possibility of interception, reprogramming, and even recombining with other genetic ensembles. For instance, a frost-resistant tomato plant is developed by separating an antifreeze gene from a cold-water flounder, a fish that can survive in very cold water, and integrating the gene into the DNA of the tomato plant cell through a bacterium, producing a new variety of tomato plant which contains a copy of the flounder antifreeze gene in every one of its cells (am I still a vegetarian when I eat that tomato?). Computer programming in its own way renders different ensembles of music, film, text, pictures, and genetic sequences readable and programmable in the common symbolic medium of binary code.

Virtual migration points to an important change in labor itself. Dominating forms of labor are concerned less and less with manipulating and altering physical objects; rather, programming allows what is in effect a liquefaction of labor, by converting different forms of work—such as architect's designs, the processing of insurance claims, animation, manufacturing designs—into code that can flow online. As a disembodied flow of signs and symbols, the code marks a transformation that has many implications for the politics of migration as well as invisible vulnerabilities that accompany the silent change. Although the global economy still produces steel and aluminum, the majority of labor, especially in the United States, has shifted to the manipulation of symbols. In a marriage of code and capital, labor increasingly moves in this code-based transnational space. Thus virtual migration attempts a shift in orientation by permitting us to talk about labor migration as more than a conventional flow of laboring bodies across national borders. This understanding raises many questions: Who protects workers in the transnational order of labor? Can national governments still provide labor protection when workers are increasingly integrated to, and dependent on, a transnational regime of code? The integration achieved through code in some ways resembles global financial integration. The decline in the demand for labor in the United States, for example, can directly influence the employment situation in India. Likewise, the ability to shift work outside the United States with relative ease, because of the universal accessibility of data servers to workers in India, increases the possibility of job displacements and layoffs in the United States.

By focusing on India and the United States I do not wish to reify "national" spaces; transnational programming schemes are not dependent on the nation-state as a unit, because telecommuting and other processes that integrate labor take place within and without the domain of nation, providing—to put it in corporate terms—"solutions and services companies need to eliminate enterprise boundaries and participate in a global marketplace" ("MySap" 2001). In this code-enabled space of transnational work, territory does not disappear or lose significance. Bangalore, Silicon Valley, and Delhi, as physical spaces of organization, turn out to be highly important, even as programming code becomes the primary ground of integration.

Since any analysis that pretends to cover global transformations has traces of conceit, it is important, even necessary, to set limits on the project. My focus is limited to the geographies of India and the United States. Boundaries of empirical discussion are even narrower: a comparative analysis of two specific labor practices—physical and virtual labor migration—with much of the analysis devoted to practices of programming and their effects. When I began this project in 1995, practices of body shopping as well as the corresponding development of offshore, online programming businesses in India were still in their infancy. Initially I began inquiring whether online services were replacing on-site work, making the physical migration of programming labor redundant, a legacy of the industrial past when labor needed to move in person. During further investigations, especially interviews, I realized that the situation was a bit more complex, though the research question was still valid. Both practices were part of the growing transnational system of flexible labor supply. Although practices of virtual migration have kept growing at a faster rate than physical migration in recent years, most Indian firms mix the two practices to achieve optimum results. Also, there were sudden spurts in physical migration during 1998–2000, when American companies needed quick solutions for their potential Y2K troubles. To disentangle the intricacies of the two practices, I conducted eighteen months of ethnographic field research—twelve months in Delhi, Gurgaon, and Noida in India and six months in New Jersey—in 1999–2000 (see appendix A for detail). The most insidious and slippery problems of such research are to escape the categories and assumptions of informants; to disentangle relevant issues from corporate discourse, which is hardwired within the paradigm of *progress* and *market*; and, as noted above, to avoid conflating the economic with the social. This is a difficult task when one is reminded that a "developing" nation like India has enormously gained, and will continue to gain, from programs of economic globalization. One must not deny India's remarkable and sorely needed economic growth in recent years. Yet one must keep an eye on the social (and environmental) costs of the global rush, especially when the social world seems almost always subordinated and assimilated to economic imperatives; I discuss some of these implications in chapters 3, 4, and 5.

In chapter 2 I attempt to situate virtual migration in the context of social theory and debates about globalization and migration. This chapter identifies two fault lines in globalization debates. The first is over whether globalization is the continuation of old trends or is something entirely new. The second is over the empirical issue of *globalization versus internationalization*; that is, whether contemporary trends reflect real globalization over and above the nation-states, or merely point out a more intensified networking of nation-states that are active participants in projects of globalization. I suggest a third way out of these dilemmas. Instead of approaching the issue from the perspective of either the global or the national, I view it in terms of numerous programs of integration that use different techniques and technologies to expand the field of governance. In a way the nation-state itself was a product of such technical powers of integration, especially when the colonizing techniques of census, post, telegraph, and railway not only turned places like India into tightly integrated societies but also made it possible to talk about such places as nation-states. The increasing labor flows—with or without the body—are part of this drive to integration.

In chapter 3 I analyze body shopping as an innovative and flexible technique of supplying programmers across national borders. The success of body shopping is in part due to the programmers' being universal, as opposed to specific, kinds of workers, as their services are required in all types of workplaces. Body shopping combines this universal characteristic of programmers with just-in-time techniques as applied to labor supply. Just as Japanese employers reduced inventories by scheduling small, precise deliveries of parts and supplies to be made by vendors *just in time*, body shopping reduces the need for a large, permanent work force by supplying programming labor just in time—when companies require it. Despite this flexibility, body shopping still requires actual border crossings through physical migration and must negotiate national boundaries and bureaucracies. With the invention of virtual labor supplies, techniques of transnational governance seem to be fast overcoming problems associated with the shipping of bodies across national spaces.

Chapter 4 focuses upon what I term the "virtual migration" of labor from India to the United States. I discuss its many features to bring to light this emerging global regime of labor integration, which has specific effects on people's social worlds. Among the many facets of virtual labor flows are a constant transnational connectivity between the client in the United States and the software company in India. Although virtual labor flows now cover programming labor as well as other forms of labor that can be provided by phone and e-mail, all services eventually rely on software applications that make instant information available to workers sitting in India. Programming in this context emerges as a universal horizon, which must always be already there if the virtual regime is to operate.

Migration literature is vast, embracing both macro perspectives, which emphasize the structural causes and functions of immigrant labor for advanced economies, and micro perspectives, such as the "push" and "pull" theory of migration. Yet with the growth of code-enabled integration, there are new empirical and theoretical challenges facing migration research. Recent technological advances have generated a curious phenomenon—the textualization (Zuboff 1988) and linguistification (Aneesh 2001) of work through software systems. The resulting dematerialization of work, which can now be textually controlled through software, reduces the need for the on-site presence of the body to perform work. Economic migration can no longer be seen purely in terms of physical human movement. With a discussion of the invisible processes of virtual migration, I attempt to provide a new conceptual framework for the prevailing immigration debates raging in the United States.

In chapter 5 I explore how programming has emerged as the most important dimension of virtual migration. Perhaps we may describe the present age as the Age of Programming in addition to using epithets such as Network Society and Information Society. As work increasingly becomes a problem of coding, and a greater number of everyday devices are embedded with the Boolean logic of programming, there is another dimension of organizational governance that adds to the already existing structures of governance reflected in *bureaucratic* forms of power (rule of the office) and *panoptic* forms of power (rule of the gaze, or surveillance). I call this algocratic governance, or the rule of code. It is in this context that virtual migration—which is above all a flow of codes, signs, and texts—becomes even more meaningful for the emerging transnational programmability, and thus governability, of processes. The contribution of this work to the literature on *organizations* consists in identifying the role of programming in *organizing* the organization. By connecting a number of globally dispersed units (such as airlines or banks) through universally accessible software systems, programming practices have enabled the same organization to exist in many places without losing its organizational structure, which is partly embedded in the system itself. Programming has also added another dimension to organizational governance by sequencing and embedding possible choices in the system, that is, by technologically coding power structures in various applications.

Chapter 6 brings the subject of code closer to that of capital by thinking of code as money in terms of symbolic constitution and social effects. Just as money establishes the rule of equivalence by expressing qualitatively different commodities in numbers, different images, animations, sounds, architectures, and even machines have become expressible in code. In short, both money and code are "global" in that they both provide liquidity to labor and merchandise through symbolization. Code and modern money, though anchored in institutional agreements and standards, follow the symbolic logic of placelessness and unfasten the ties that bind things to particular sites. The idea of virtual migration derives from this semiotic transformation of labor, from the code-based convertibility of labor. This transformation is also rooted, as I pointed out earlier, in a general, code-based knowledge formation that characterizes fields ranging from biology to computer science. Just as code and money provide a basis for equivalence and liquidity among qualitatively different commodities, genetic code becomes the language of biological organisms whose differences become expressible in the sequencing of its letters. The last chapter attempts to link the discussion of code and virtual migration back to the issues of nation, state, capital, and globalization.

The last few decades have witnessed extensive technological transformations in production and work. These changes do more than influence how work is organized within the national boundaries; they also have transnational ramifications. This book attempts to provide a new angle for exploring this global shift in terms of a specific transnational practice—online virtual labor across national spaces—that informs debates transcending the site and nature of this specific work practice. Another contribution that I hope to make is to provide information about a phenomenon on which little sociological literature is available: the intersection and reciprocal influences of "third world" identity, programming technologies, and transnational labor markets, an intersection that makes India a particularly interesting site for research.

CHAPTER 2

Programming Globalization: Visions and Revisions

At the beginning of the twenty-first century, anxious concerns about glob-alization arose not from any place considered part of the "third world" but surprisingly from the land of free trade: the United States. It was on the misty streets of Seattle, a quiet and high-tech metropolis, that the drama reached its loud and unsettling expression. In late 1999, during the meetings of the World Trade Organization (WTO), tear gas, plastic bullets, and pepper spray were aimed at the citizens of the "first world." Street protests forced the mayor of Seattle to impose a curfew and declare the first state of emergency in the city since the 1960s, while the governor of Washington called in the National Guard. The larger context of this event was globalization.

In recent years, many organizations such as the International Forum on Globalization (IFG), Direct Action Network (DAN), and Friends of the Earth International have been formed to mobilize public opinion against the forces of globalization. Most anti-globalization forums—contrary to their stated aims—seem to advocate greater and more specific globalization. While seek-ing to "*reverse* the globalization process by encouraging ideas and activities which revitalize local economies and communities, and ensure long term ecological stability" (International Forum on Globalization 2001), many anti-globalization programs are deeply implicated in the globalization dis-course by striving to establish a global ethic based on universal human rights, workers' rights, and environmental protection.[1] Environmental movements, with concerns ranging from rain forests to the butterfly effects of environ-mental damage,[2] are global in their approach; they also demand global inter-vention, seeing the earth as a material limit on consumption. Similarly, labor unions in the United States, even while trying to protect the local labor force from a global onslaught of trade and migration, seek to make workers' rights globally binding on all nations. The president of the AFL-CIO, John

Sweeney—advocating a specific kind of globalization—called upon "the delegates to the World Trade Organization to address workers' rights and human rights as well as environmental and consumer protections in the rules that govern the global economy." The language of rights can indeed be a very effective tool for promoting social justice in different sociocultural contexts. But one must also realize that the universal juridical nature of "global" rights is also an effective means to harmonize conflicting interests and approaches, and thus prepare a level playing field on which economic globalization can take place. The rights-based unification of the world is comparable to monetary unification, which also requires, as with the European Union, efforts to bring all members together on a feasible economic plane.

Curiously, the interests of the state and of protesters, despite the police crackdown in Seattle, were not totally at odds. Amid skepticism and disapproval by the heads of developing nations,[3] President Bill Clinton signed a treaty committing the United States to international laws that ban the worst forms of child labor. For developing nations, the idea of linking global trade with local labor standards amounted to protectionism by the developed world, a device by which rich nations could impose tariffs on imports from the developing countries, accusing them of unfair labor practices when it suited their economy.

Perhaps the real concern of labor unions was neither human rights violations nor the harsh working and living conditions in other countries. Those conditions had existed long before "globalization" even emerged as an object of analysis. Rather, the problem was the destabilizing conditions of labor and livelihood in the United States produced by the transformations generally described as globalization. No wonder Sweeney, in the same speech about human rights violations in China, shifted his concern to the fear of job losses: "For working families in this country, the global economy is not an abstraction. Many jobs are dependent on exports. Many are lost to imports. Employers routinely use the threat to move abroad as a club in contract negotiations. Even with the economy growing, the most efficient steelworkers in the world [in Pittsburgh] saw their jobs swept away by a flood of dumped imports" (Sweeney 1999).

The question of labor and livelihood became a more direct concern in 2004. With a couple of million jobs lost in the United States during

George W. Bush's presidency, virtual migration—under the broader economic term *outsourcing*—became a dark symbol of globalization, and an instant target of attack by the Democrats in election-year politics. For economists there is nothing disconcerting about either trade or outsourcing; they would point out that trade helps more than it hurts, citing cases from Asia and Africa (Bhagwati 2004). Outsourcing, according to N. Gregory Mankiw, chairman of Bush's Council of Economic Advisors, is "just a new way of doing international trade. More things are tradable than were tradable in the past. And that's a good thing." Although Mankiw's comments caused a furor amid the general anxiety over the shipping of jobs to India and China, there is nothing remarkable about his statement. In economic theory, when a service is produced at lower cost by another firm or country, it makes no economic sense to produce it domestically; outsourcing allows corporations to devote their resources to more productive purposes. If the 1990s are any evidence, the biggest increase in job creation occurred in the United States during the rise of the regime of virtual labor migration, which some would have expected to result in reduced job growth because of the supposed shipping of work overseas. If job growth in the United States in the 1990s was not attributable to the Indian IT industry, then neither can one fairly attribute more recent job losses to it.

How do we think of the concerns of labor unions or other anti-globalists? These concerns must be more than mere attempts to make China or India a scapegoat for domestic problems. To my understanding, the concerns are minor revolts against the continuous assimilation of the social to the economic. Job displacements, endless demands for retraining, perceived job insecurity, and the demand of continuous flexibility by a growing "flexible" economic system have escalated disruptions in the social realm. The increasing functional integration of the world economy produces real and imagined perceptions of social vulnerability. For example, the digitization of finance has made financial disinvestments and withdrawals from national economies extremely easy, while also creating new vulnerabilities by making people's lives and livelihood dependent on the transnational investor's panic and perception. A good case in point is the Asian crisis of the 1990s, when the flight of capital turned the nation-states involved into observers of their own economic breakdown. The more thoroughly integrated an economy is into global ebbs and flows, the more vulnerable are people's social worlds. Econo-mists try to calm fears by saying that global integration may result in job losses and disruptions only in the short run; in the long run, with the help of education and the retooling of the workforce, the economy is bound to gain. One may invoke John Maynard Keynes's well-known quote: "In the long run we are all dead" (and some are dead even in the short run if "IMF suicides" among workers who lost their jobs and dignity during the Asian crisis are any indication). Perhaps jobs do tend to return, at least in a better-managed economy. But they do not appear in the sectors where they were lost. After all, the protests in Seattle took place during the zenith of the American econ-omy. To labor unions, however, the jobs gained in the information economy did not help the people who lost in the manufacturing sector, unless of course they had reeducated and reskilled themselves for the new economy. Social disruption is systemic even during times of economic gain. Economists are right in one respect: work created in other countries does not diminish the prospect of job growth at home and may even enhance it. According to a report by the consulting firm McKinsey (2004), the United States captures 78 percent of the total value created globally by all outsourcing while the receiving countries get only 22 percent. Obviously investors in the United States gain; so do consumers, through lower prices. Unless the welfare state returns, however, the economic gains cannot be diverted toward relocation benefits and social welfare to reduce the pain of social disruption in laboring lives. Capital does tend to gain more than labor.

From this chaos, one conclusion is obvious: "globalization" as an object of analysis offers a complex, interesting, and conflicting array of possibili-ties, in which states, labor unions, environmental groups, and local grassroots organizations are all transnational players. In this ever-expanding field of transnational governance, labor unions and other anti-globalization groups in the United States—which insist on the global implementation of human rights—seem to be demanding more, and not less, global governance. Re-sistance to the global order of things also becomes global, reflected in such slogans as the "globalization of justice." We live in a world where specu-lative flows of finance capital have surpassed global trade and become un-hinged from the flow of real resources (see for example Singh 1999). We live in a world where volatile financial flows—attracted by short-term speculative gains (Soros 1998) — compel national states to pursue monetary and fiscal policies that conform to the interests of global finance capital in increasingly complex networks (Castells 1996, 102–6). We live in a world where trade is composed disproportionately of intrafirm transactions and services. As John Ruggie (1993) puts it: "[It is not] clear what it means to say that services are traded. In merchandise trade, factors of production stand still and goods move across borders; in traded services, typically the factors of production do the moving while the good (service) stands still: it is produced for the consumer on the spot." We also live in a world where certain forms of labor — as I will discuss later in detail — can move on line without the body. Such progressive integration of the world is a matter of heated debates around the contested term "globalization." A brief look at these debates will facilitate a clearer understanding of current transformations.

Despite a consensus about accelerated flows of capital and commodities across state borders, debates on globalization reveal strong disagreement. Most discussions tend to split along two fault lines: one over historical continuity (whether the present form of globalization is a qualitatively new phenomenon or a mere continuation of world historical capitalism) and the other over the importance of the nation-state (whether globalization is a phenomenon that transcends national states or is only an effect of relationships among national states). After a brief discussion of these debates, I will attempt an analysis of globalization in terms of forms or schemes of integration to overcome the dilemmas of old versus new and national versus global.

Historical Continuity or
Contingent Turns of History

Those who view globalization as a historical continuation of capitalist expansion may cite Marx's writings of more than a century ago: "The need of a constantly expanding market for its products chases the bourgeoisie [transnational capitalist class, or TCC] over the whole surface of the globe. It must nestle everywhere, settle everywhere, establish connections everywhere . . . The bourgeoisie [TCC], by the rapid improvement of all instruments of production, by the immensely facilitated means of communication, draws all . . . nations into civilisation. The cheap prices of its commodities are the heavy artillery with which it batters down all Chinese walls . . . It compels all nations, on pain of extinction, to adopt the bourgeois [capitalistic] mode of production; it compels them to introduce what it calls civilisation into their midst, i.e., to become bourgeois [capitalistic] themselves. In one word, it creates a world after its own image" (Marx and Engels 1985, 83–84). Hence one may argue that globalization is a new label for a relatively old process. Practitioners of world-systems research—who follow the work of Immanuel Wallerstein (1974), and who may well claim that ideas of globalization owe their wide currency to their method of viewing the whole world as a system of relationships—have long documented the dynamics of an expanding capitalist world economy (see for example Arrighi 1994; Chase-Dunn 1998; Wallerstein 1974). Others argue that present-day electronic systems are a continuation of early-twentieth-century transaction techniques using submarine international telegraph cable (Hirst and Thompson 1996).

Many others, however, maintain that globalization is a relatively new phenomenon, a result of developments in capitalism since the 1960s (Sklair 1999) or of late modernity (Giddens 1990; Spybey 1996). Martin Albrow (1997), on the other hand, attempts to understand the global age without referring to the modernist language of "new" and "old." Treating the present age as discontinuous from the past, he argues that modernist accounts of the present era—couched in such familiar categories as world order, global culture, late modernity—can never allow us to enter a different age, since they must narrate the future as a continuation of past trends. The question of continuity and change brings us back to the problem I discussed earlier: the problem of a trans-historical constant that has traversed the entire length of history without changing itself. The subject of continuity inevitably leads to the question: The continuity of *what*, or alternatively, the emergence of *what* and within *what* framework? Are we talking about the continuity of capitalism or globalization, if either, when we discuss these processes? Even researchers who fall on the same side of the debate may be talking about the continuity of different things. Unlike Hirst and Thompson, who advocate the continuity of "international" or interstate processes, some scholars may not regard the world economy as an interstate economy with discrete national economic spaces. Following Marx, some see nation-states as mere jurisdictional claims in a unitary world market (Arrighi, Hopkins, and Wallerstein 1989).

In many ways, globalization resembles oxygen. I do not mean that it helps us to breathe better. The discovery of globalization is more like the discovery of oxygen in the sense discussed by Kuhn (1962, 53–56). It is hard to say when oxygen was discovered. Was oxygen discovered when Priestley isolated a gas, though impure, that was later recognized as a distinct type? He did not recognize it *as* oxygen, whose properties were later understood a little better, though still not completely, by Lavoisier among others. Kuhn maintains that the question is not about a particular piece of reality per se but about the way scientists think about it. As far as descriptions and understanding were concerned, Priestley and Lavoisier were not talking about exactly the same gas, because "when paradigms change, the world itself changes with them," and one must learn to see a "new gestalt" to inhabit the new world (Kuhn 1962). Reality is not something that takes place behind the back of languages, discourses, and instruments; rather, the real is actively produced by them in a strange circularity. One could say that oxygen has always existed independent of its discovery. But has it? Until people were able to extract and define what it was, did it "really" exist for us who were just happy breathing air? If it did, then we must agree that there is a lot of reality waiting to be discovered through innumerable known as well as unknown knowledge frameworks; that is, a form of reality exists which is not yet real enough to be called real in any real sense. But possibilities are not realities (some day even the ghosts as seen by some might be empirically verified by means of agreement on the definition of a ghost and finding one; I would be hesitant to call ghosts real just yet). We can perhaps discuss oxygen not as an unchanging reality (i.e., outside time), anterior to both concepts and precepts, that has continued since the Big Bang but as the product of a sophisticated way of thinking about and producing the world in a dense gathering of different concepts (atom, molecule, pressure, gas, temperature). Globalization too is perhaps a new way of thinking and talking about the world. Discourses of globalization may help us not only to explain some events in the past but also to produce future events in specific directions. My own contribution to the globalization discourse relates not to the big question of whether globalization is new or old but to a different, if not a new, way of looking at certain forms of integration. This brings us to arguments around the second fault line in globalization debates: whether globalization is a phenomenon separate from internationalization.

Globalization versus Internationalization

Although there is no single definition of globalization, there is a consensus among some scholars that it is no longer adequate to study contemporary issues at the level of national states, using state-centered models (Albrow 1997; Johnston 1982; Ohmae 1985; Ohmae 1999; Robertson 1992; Sklair 1995; Sklair 1998). Such globalists argue that a combination of global economic institutions, transnational corporations, and globalizing ideologies drastically undermine the historical primacy of the nation-state as the regulator of its national economy. Despite broad agreement among globalists, they do not reflect an unbroken unity, as Sklair (1999) has identified four separate research clusters within globalization studies: the world-systems approach, the global culture approach, the global society approach, and the global capitalism approach.

Many scholars resist and question the notion of globalization itself. They stress that nation-states gain even more importance as they strive to enhance their strengths to compete globally with other national economies; they are the source of the skills and technologies that underpin competitive advantage (Porter 1990). In fact, the world economy, some argue, may be less well integrated now than it was during the classical era of the gold standard (Drache and Boyer 1996), and less global and expansive than it was during the age of world empires (Weiss 1998). Hirst and Thompson (1992; 1996) call globalization, as conceived by the more extreme globalists, a myth. They argue that the world economy is still an "international" economy in which national economies act as its primary units. They point out the weak development of true TNCs (transnational corporations) and the continuing significance of MNCs (multinational corporations), regulated through nation-states, guided by national labor regulations, and protected by the military (especially when operating abroad), with clear national headquarters. Behind these arguments lies a genuine concern: "One key effect of the concept of globalization has been to paralyse radical reforming national strategies, to see them as unfeasible in the face of the judgment and sanction of international markets. If, however, we face economic changes that are more complex and more equivocal than the extreme globalists argue, then the possibility remains of political strategy and action for national and international control of market economies in order to promote social goals" (Hirst and Thompson 1996, 1). A related concern is shown by others who view globalization as a self-fulfilling prophecy of the neoliberal program: "neo-liberalism . . . is an intrinsically globalizing project . . . [opposed] to each and every territorial and political constraint on markets . . ." (Scott 1997, 11). To these scholars globalization is not an autonomous process that undermines the ability of nation-states to protect against the deregulation of their markets. In fact the nation-state— under contemporary neoliberal pressures—is the key actor in effecting deregulation both internally by privatization and externally by membership in international associations such as GATT (Scott 1997).

In step with the view that globalization is not necessarily a process in opposition to the nation-state, I attempt a more concrete way out of the duality of the "global" and the "national" by looking at globalization processes as programs of integration, or acts of programming, to which the relative importance of national versus global institutions is less relevant. The dichotomy of the global and the national implicitly relies on constructions of the *state* as a governing "body," an "actor" with coherent interests, motives, and action, directed toward or against larger *global* forces. Although a number of studies have recently exposed and questioned the reified notions of both "nation" (Anderson 1991; Balibar and Wallerstein 1991; Brubaker 1996; Calhoun 1997; Handler 1988; Hobsbawm 1992; Malkki 1995) and "state" (Cox 1997; Ferguson 1999; Latham 2000; Ruggie 1993), the use of nation-states as units and instruments of analysis is common. Analyses that take the unity of nation-states and national economies for granted—quite valuable in certain contexts—fall on both sides of the debate. On the globalization side, studies demonstrate the decline of the nation-state by showing its compromised sovereignty in the face of globalizing forces. By contrast, others show the continued, or even growing, importance of the nation-state in the global system.

One way to steer away from the duality of the global and the national is to view the nation-state as a bundle of countless, sometimes competing, programs, techniques, mechanisms, rationalities, and discourses employed and institutionalized for governance. It is obvious that neither is the coupling of "nation" and "state" as tight and natural as previously imagined, nor does the state have the coherent consciousness of an actor. Indeed, the world polity is relatively stateless in view of common models of scripted social orders—

models of economic development, human rights, education, national identity—that have become authoritative in many social settings (Meyer 2000) and define the nation-state system while remaining outside the boundaries of any given nation-state (Meyer 1980). In this view, the nation-state is actualized through a set of governance practices, which in fact may not be limited to the nation-state alone. As Max Weber (1978) had earlier noted, rational techniques and "legal-rational" methods of governance were essential to modern state practices as well as to various private and public bureaucracies. The modern state itself was only a part of this emerging science of governance, which employed a new economy of techniques and technologies, and embedded authority not in the person of the king or president but in positions, rules, and law. With this understanding of the state, national and global agencies do not necessarily belong to two separate realms; rather, both are inseparable parts of ever-growing and refined practices of national and transnational governance, or what I call *programming schemes*.

The term "programming" here is used in its broadest sense; computer programming is but a small part of the whole gamut of programming schemes. The *Oxford English Dictionary* defines the word "programming" in four senses: *scheduling* or *arrangement* of content (as in television programming); *planning* in the economic sense (administration, control, or management); computer *programming*, or the use of coded orders to communicate with the machine; and *conditioning* in the psychological sense (an instruction method). Combining these different senses, we may understand programming schemes as scripts of governance or productive control. Ranging from scripts embedded in automatic teller machines (ATMs) that guide our transaction step by step, to traffic models that distribute trips by combining data on road networks and on socioeconomic habits (e.g., people would travel farther to get to work than to pick up a pizza), programming schemes may be characterized as purposive, integrative, productive, and simulative. Programming schemes animate not only state institutions—both capitalist and socialist—but also corporate and nongovernmental organizations. Later, in chapter 5, I discuss programming schemes in three clusters, setting up the world for specific types of governance: bureaucratic, panoptic, and algocratic.

The proliferation of programming schemes in recent decades is part of a more general war on surprise. From state planning, corporate management, and risk management to genetic modifications of plant and animal life, the endeavor to bring everything into the realm of governance and productivity has intensified over the years. Efforts are on, irrespective of the chances of success, to improve the human brain with cognitive enhancement drugs now under development in neuropharmacological research; these drugs will presumably improve memory by influencing how neurons encode long-term memories, and "allow normal individuals to sleep less, work harder and play more" (Hall 2003).[4] It is not just the control of disease that is important; "just as exciting is the possibility that healthy individuals might become 'better than well'" through lifestyle drugs that would program how their brains protect and grow neurons (Gage 2003). To defeat the human tendency to deceive others, efforts are being made to develop brain-imaging machines or functional magnetic resonance imaging (fMRI) techniques that would follow human thought processes more closely than polygraph tests, which measure only such indirect signs as pulse, skin conductance, and respiratory rate. Further, GPS navigation technologies are being devised for purposes ranging from tracking every step of a "sexual predator" released from prison (Haddock 2004) to guiding the blind (Prince 2004) and conquering the road.

Programming schemes are not necessarily successful schemes. Disasters—natural and social—continue to happen. At times, disaster planning schemes serve merely ritualistic and symbolic functions without much chance of being effective (Clarke 1999). But the question of failure itself suggests the existence of prior schemes of control that failed. The fantasy of control is at least as important as control itself. There are two aspects of the dynamic of productive control that I will discuss here, linking it later to the question of the national-global divide. First, integrations brought about by schemes of governance tend to introduce new risks and uncertainties, and thus create the requirement of additional controls. Second, programming schemes at once bring about integration along the new plane and prompt the disintegration of earlier orders. To understand this dynamic, two examples from colonial India, regarding railway and postal networks, will help.

To control the vast region of the Indian subcontinent, the introduction of railway and postal systems was necessary for the British colonial enterprise. Lord Dalhousie, the governor general of the East India Company, recognized the usefulness of railways for imperial governance when he wrote in 1853: "A single glance cast upon the map recalling to mind the vast extend of the Empire we hold . . . will suffice to show how immeasurable are the political advantages to be derived from a system of internal communication which would admit of full intelligence of every event being transmitted to the Government under all circumstance, at a speed exceeding five-fold its present rate" (Prakash 1999). Railway construction in the subcontinent started in 1850, and by 1883 a basic trunk system and some feeder lines were in place, for a total route mileage of 10,198; by 1903 India's railway, "the network of iron sinew"[5] with over 25,000 route miles, was the fourth-largest in the world (Kerr 1995). Because of their sheer complexity and vastness, such schemes of integration give rise to many uncertainties and risks, requiring another set of controls along administrative lines. As Chandler (1977) demonstrates regarding American railroads, there developed multiple layers of management and a whole range of bureaucratic techniques, including organizational charts showing lines of authority and communication, to control and coordinate numerous geographically dispersed units.

This systemic integration of the Indian subcontinent through the railways brings us to the second point about a partial disappearance, for good or bad, of earlier forms of social integration organized around, for example, caste hierarchies and notions of ritual pollution and untouchability. As caste lacked identifiable marks of race or the payment capacity of class, its hierarchy could not easily be sustained on train compartments. This point will become clearer in my discussion of the postal system, which again served the need acutely felt by the British East India Company for regular and reliable means of communication.

The postal system—that "Grand Victorian Technology," to borrow a phrase from Chattopadhyay (2004)—introduced, even more than the railway network, a different scheme of place, carried right up to people's doorsteps. From the establishment of three post offices by the East India Company in Calcutta, Bombay, and Madras in 1766 to the introduction of the PIN (Postal Index Number) after independence, postal geography integrated the subcontinent along the new logic of circles, regions, divisions, and PIN codes. It introduced rational maps of the landscape and techniques of letter switching at the post office. In the postal switching system, quite like the store-and-forward system of Internet protocols, a letter is not taken directly from source to destination; rather, it is taken temporarily to a post office where a large number of letters and packets are gathered and sorted for each delivery route before starting their journey to the delivery post office closer to the destination. Standardized addressing was another aspect of these schemes of postal communication, which while integrating the colony also brought about a certain disintegration in previous ways of locating and addressing. One was no longer supposed to address a letter to "Dinesh's Father with a house by the pond behind the Neem tree where cattle are kept." The postal address was now required to be unique and unambiguous, and also part of the postal matrix. The introduction of this form of addressing did not mean that it was successfully implemented: the failure in producing a completely depersonalized and formal space may still be noticed in a small number of postal addresses — originating specifically from villages — that defy all abstract logic, to the vexation of postal employees in India.

The railway and postal schemes of integration, even if institutionally organized around national territory, are neither national nor global. In fact, it was a transnational private company that transformed India into a modern nation-state through these schemes of integration. The British East India Company was the first to colonize parts of the Indian subcontinent in the eighteenth century, leading to the formation of modern states in South Asia. The transformation of the subcontinent into a system of modern nation-states was made possible by such schemes of integrative governance as censuses, maps, railways, and post and telegraph networks, which unified each nation-state's geography and provided its people with a new, integrated framework. In an important sense, therefore, the modern nation-state itself was made possible through the programming schemes and associated technologies of administration, which imposed a new order on life by cataloguing, counting, and enclosing populations within newly constructed borders. Even in Europe, state-based territoriality emerged only after judicial, administrative, constabulary, and military techniques had been deployed for centuries (Latham 2000).

These schemes of governance simultaneously integrated communal life on a scale much larger than had been possible earlier, and devised new surveillance and disciplinary techniques to manage the resulting chaos. Thus, the modern "nation-state" resulted from a technological takeoff in governance.

While the "nation" part of the nation-state was actualized through various technologies that facilitated the social imagination of the nation through different media—print languages, radio, and television (Anderson 1991)—the state was made possible through the systemic integration achieved by the abstract logic of administrative schemes as well as the steering media of national currency.

The modern nation-state expresses a more specific kind of integration, however: the constitution of the social world as a system of enclosures through strict national borders, or governance by enclosing objects of control and intervention. As a unit of governance, the reified reality of the nation-state comes into being through the logic and regime of what I call total closure, bringing into unity the twin dimensions of *peoplehood* and *territoriality*. The first dimension, tapping into the archaic core of what Durkheim calls collective conscience, creates a particular style of subjectivity (nationalism), whereas the dimension of territoriality helps to ground the nation-state in precise geography with a view to attaining an effective, functional, and governable whole.

The Modern Nation-State and Total Closure

The model of the nation-state—at its most general level—is a model of boundaries. There seems to be no consistency among different nations in terms of *what* binds them together, or *what* they claim as the basis and essence of their nationhood, which lends itself to different definitions in different contexts (e.g., religion, language, ethnicity); but there is remarkable correspondence in how these communities close their boundaries and how they structure and legitimate their enclosures. The logic behind boundary construction is that of total closure, organizing a twofold collective orientation. First, total closure helps to mark all the members in a constructed enclosure as identical, dedifferentiating them in terms of their "identity." For example, all citizens of India become "Indians" endowed with an essential collective identity, regardless of the internal variation within the total enclosure thus constituted. Second, total closure creates a sharp, unbridgeable gulf from other groups, as is true of the homogenizing category of Pakistanis. This closure may or may not be an institutionalized closure, as reflected in the nationalist bent of such separatist movements as those of Quebec, Jaffna, Punjab, and Chechnya, which seek to break away and form their own closure. It is perhaps expedient to distinguish the non-institutionalized total closure as the *nation* and the institutionalized total closure as the *state*. While *nation* harbors the idea of single peoplehood, *state* is a structure of governance that realizes the idea of total closure. The nation-state in its hyphenated form combines the idea of one peoplehood with institutionalized structures of closure, each securing the truth of the other. Here the term "total" does not describe reality per se, as all closures are "contingent" in the last analysis (Böröcz 1997b); it only expresses a particular constitution and understanding of reality.

Territoriality emerges as an inseparable component of the modern nation-state. As the model of total closure is applied to the territorial basis of nations, it is not surprising that national frontiers seem to surpass in rigidity all previous communal boundaries. Unlike the loose, fuzzy territorial limits of earlier communities, such as dynastic realms, or empires, where borders faded and territories merged indiscernibly into one another (Anderson 1991), the boundaries of nations rigidly demarcate one cluster of regions and populations from another, and also cut up the sky and the sea into exclusive national spaces. Border patrolling, border fencing, and ports of entry, combined with a constant vigil against the slightest border violations, impart to the national frontier an immovable rigidity. In view of constant border disputes throughout the world, nothing appears more arbitrary than national boundaries; yet there is no other boundary system that evokes greater awe, or arouses a stronger shock.

The maintenance of rigid, sharp, unyielding boundaries is characterized by an either/or logic of total closure, a logic of inclusion or exclusion, lumping supposedly homogeneous chunks of identity and splitting them off from one another as discrete entities (Zerubavel 1991), thereby partitioning the globe into insular national ghettos. The result is that migration emerges as a problem in the era of modern nation-states. The logic of total closure and associated practices construct categories of inclusion, such as the "citizen" or the "resident"; at the same time they constitute categories of "exclusion" — the alien, the immigrant, the refugee. When the United States was still to become a nation, the people migrating to the "new world" did not face the prospect of being termed illegal aliens, as there was no fixed "national cast" that would make it possible to construct the category of outcasts. When the new form of governance organized "total" national enclosures, it also produced categories of people that spilled over the framework, such as illegal aliens and refugees, who became objects of either derision or compassion depending on the circumstances. Just as pure conceptions of the body produced dangerously anomalous categories of excreta, saliva, rheum, and genital secretions, usually despised for falling into a gray zone outside the sacred domain of the body (Douglas 1978), the conception of the "nation" as a sacrosanct body gave rise to "problems" or "anomalies" to be solved by national governments, which may in fact have been responsible for the rise of the categories in the first place. A good example is the emergence of the refugee, who did not exist in the modern sense before the order of nations (Malkki 1995). Before the advent of nations and their political and legal cast, which makes deviant categories possible, there were only gypsies, nomads, and settlers, who entered into local power relations without rituals of strict documentation (visas, fingerprinting, or oaths of allegiance). People, like birds, migrated from harsher climates to balmy ones. The emergence of total national enclosures became the condition of the very possibility of the refugee and the alien.

During the seventeenth and eighteenth centuries, when the United States was only a nascent nation, immigration was relatively unhindered. No national action could be taken until the Civil War, when Congress created the *office* of commissioner of immigration. It was not until the 1880s that the United States began to enact major immigration laws, targeting at first immigrants who could be excluded from the American self-conception of nationhood. The Chinese Exclusion Act of 1882 was an early sign of change from the previous practice of open immigration. Even in 1893 there were only two immigration ports of entry along the border, one of which was perhaps at El Paso. Six years later, in 1899, there were only four immigration inspectors functioning along the Mexican border (Kurian and Harahan 1998), compared to more than nine thousand border patrol agents in 2000. It was only after the administrative integration of boundaries that one could talk of "a" nation-state with a unified national space. The strengthening of the system of the modern nation-state has indeed been the strengthening of techniques and technologies of integration. In fact, migration itself has become an object of intervention and governance schemes.

Migration and Mobility: Governing Space and Time

The drive to integrate—with refined instruments and apparatuses—itself produced conditions for extensive migration in a relatively short period in modern history. Its innovations in transport and communication carried and connected people far from their immediate locations. It fashioned integrated societies—such as India and the United States—by knitting them together with extensive railroad, postal, and highway networks. Later, air transport effected another break with the past, producing a different reality of migration and the world around us. Faster jets, ships, and trains may act as instruments of various integration schemes, which proliferate as forms of power during wars or economic crises when the need for control and domination is high. No wonder that the Second World War produced faster jets and nuclear power, and that cold war rivalry led to satellites watching the earth like hawks: at one time 40 percent of research and development effort worldwide focused on military technology (Barnaby 1981). Paul Edwards (1996) has shown how the development of computer technology in the postwar era was shaped by the tracking, targeting, communication, and integration needs of air and nuclear warfare management.

The technologies that are most closely tied to current forms of global integration—and that are part of the most important technological revolution of the second half of the twentieth century, the Internet—also owe their initial articulation to a war strategy. These origins belie the popular notion that the market is the source of all technological innovation and creativity, and thus of all forms of globalization. The U.S. Defense Advanced Research Projects Agency (DARPA) developed ARPANET, forerunner of the Internet, and the RAND Corporation, founded by the U.S. Air Force, was instrumental through the efforts of Paul Baran in conceiving the "distributed network," a network with many nodes, but with no center that could be destroyed in a nuclear attack (Abbate 1999; Baran 1964). This ingenious programming scheme of distributed communication was the basis of the Internet, which later found a commercial application in the World Wide Web—a virtually integrated globe.

One should however distinguish the reality of a materially integrated globe from that of a virtually integrated world. The second kind of integration is a reverse integration. It does not force places or people to join in dubious togetherness; it does not coerce the obstinate reality of distance into submission, nor does it compress the globe into a ball. Rather, it distributes and disperses. Indeed, it connects only through code. I will discuss the specifics of distributed programming in chapter 5 to clarify this point. For the present purpose, an example from the DARPA's Terrorist Information Awareness (TIA) program, previously called Total Information Awareness, may suffice. Although the U.S. Congress, under pressure from civil liberties groups, unfunded parts of this project, I discuss it as an example of distributed integration. The project combined many existing programming schemes that had received fresh support after the September 11 terrorist strikes. These schemes were intended to capture patterns of public and private transactions worldwide to detect early signs of disturbances in data flows, and to predict subversive acts already being planned. As an instance of distributed integration, this virtual data modeling does not forcibly join disparate entities, people, or spaces together: it only attempts to know the truth of their distribution by prompting new interrelationships to exist among heterogeneous data sets of natural languages, biometric information, and financial transactions around the globe. It is not a retrospective strategy of collecting clues about a crime after the fact; instead, it is a prospective endeavor to unearth "plausible futures" within an hour after a triggering event occurs or an articulated threshold has been passed. Automatically, queue analysts go to work based on partial pattern matches; they have at their disposal patterns that cover 90 percent of all previously known foreign terrorist attacks (Defense Advanced Research Projects Agency 2003). Various programs under TIA utilize a range of techniques, including scalable algorithms to detect and visualize social networks, automated speech and text exploitation in multiple languages, predictive modeling borrowed from the futures markets of global finance, and technologies of human identification at a distance. Virtual integration, as a form of power, mines, combines, and codes data on globally distributed sites and situations. It is also distributed integration in another, more immediate sense: it allows agents to be distributed globally in a linked network of direct collaboration for effective and immediate action.

It may be useful to distinguish between two clusters of technologies that are deployed to integrate space in different ways. The first cluster comprises technologies of *material mobility* (automobile, train, aircraft, ship) that help to surmount space by moving physical bodies and objects at high speeds, and the second, technologies of *virtual mobility* that move text, voices, and images (computer networks, phones) across enormous distances. This analytical distinction is useful for my discussion later of *body shopping*, or embodied labor migration (chapter 3), and *virtual migration*, or disembodied labor migration (chapter 4). The distinction is merely analytical because in practice both clusters of technologies exist side by side and both depend on abstract programming schemes. It is illuminating to bring out their analytical particularity, in order to understand the difference in their actual and possible deployments and effects.

Mobilities: Virtual and Material

In the last few decades, there has been a new development within technologies of virtual mobility. Unlike earlier analog technologies of phones and telegraph, recent technologies are digital. Analog signals degenerate slightly whenever they are switched from one link to another; therefore a basic rule of thumb for earlier phone systems was to minimize the number of links between source and destination. Digital signals, on the other hand, can be regenerated at each switch, and thus can keep hopping from link to link without cumulative distortion. We can capture this newly developed difference between technologies of material and virtual mobility in terms of the distinction by Negroponte (1995) between "atoms" and "bits." Technologies of material mobility are technologies of atoms, of matter. They help move objects and information in their material form, such as newspapers and books. A *bit*—despite being anchored in silicon—is immaterial in itself. Its significance lies in being a logical signal with no color, size, or weight, and it can travel at the speed of light. Like the atom, a bit is constructed as the smallest unit of information (a 1 or a 0), an abstraction from voltage fluctuations. Bits, being an actualized mathematical idea, can be symbolically manipulated, in direct contrast to atoms, which require physical governance. Being abstract, bits can be made to mix more effortlessly, as we see in the mixing of audio, video, and textual data, labeled as multimedia; this mixture may be packaged, made to travel, and then unwrapped at another end, thus constituting the possibility of virtual work flow. This fact has immense implications for the growth of virtual labor migration across the globe. The enormous flexibility achieved through the symbolic conversion of a variety of tasks into software programs brings more and more areas under the umbrella of "virtually" possible online work. With virtual mobility, a programmer's labor can move from her desk in New Delhi to a corporation's computer in New York as if they were two adjacent machine tools. A consequence of the virtual flow of labor is the reduced relevance of bodily movement across physical space, making embodied migration a less-needed activity. In computer work, information moves at the velocity of light, allowing the worker's body to stay put. Thus, technologies of virtual mobility are strategic for the migration of abstract skills without the body.

Technologies responsible for material mobility depend heavily on a material conception of space and time. We can easily see the importance of physical motion in technologies of material mobility as in large-scale material migrations all over the world. Such technologies obviously involve interaction with atoms in space, as they are deployed to move labor along with its complete material context—the body, the family, and the material location. These technologies, which allowed for incredible innovations in transport, represent the conquest of space through the physical movement of bodies—both human and manufactured. Since the eighteenth and nineteenth centuries technologies of the atom have been able to radically reduce the size of the globe as the time taken to traverse space has decreased, a phenomenon termed "time–space compression" by David Harvey (1989). Technologies of virtual mobility appear to announce the victory over space in another round of time-space compression. Rather than move the body across space, they freeze it geographically, and move immense quantities of audio-visual bytes at the speed of light across enormous distances. This has very different consequences for labor migration. Transport technologies enabled the material, face-to-face interaction of people and cultures by transporting the body, allowing for unprecedented migrations. Technologies of virtual mobility make possible an interaction through images, text, and sounds.

The contrast between technologies of material and virtual mobilities enables a conceptualization of labor flows both "with" and "without" the body, with the physical presence of the worker and with only the worker's virtual presence. It therefore opens an analytical realm of inquiry into migration, employment, and transnational programming schemes from a new angle, with the possibility of bringing diverse areas and explanations together under a sociology of borders and flows (Böröcz 1997). The power of the modern nation-state has relied largely on its ability to control the material mobility of labor, shutting and opening its borders according to its needs. As a system of enclosures, it has the necessary force to stop or to allow the physical flow of goods or labor across its heavily guarded boundaries. However, physical borders are less useful against virtual mobility. Although walls can be raised even against virtual mobility by disallowing material anchors like computers and other physical equipment, or by legislating within the national territory against the use of necessary bandwidth, such measures in fact reduce the power of the state by robbing it of the possibility to govern virtual flows and hence reap financial gains. Thus technologies of virtual mobility—as part of transnational programming schemes—increasingly require the fine-tuning of the existing institutional organization if the nation-state is to retain its power of governance. But not only do practices of material migration continue to grow—in addition, their governance has become a major issue around the world. A brief examination of immigration debates in the United States will bring out the continued importance of material migration, while permitting an instructive contrast with what I call "virtual migration."

The debate whether the United States as a nation-state (implying a certain closure around its people and territory) stands to gain or lose from immigrant workers—in terms of economic, fiscal, demographic, or cultural consequences—has been intensifying for some time (Edmonston and Smith 1997; Espenshade 1996; Friedberg and Hunt 1995). Lately, a large demand and influx of information technology (IT) workers has forced the debate to enter the high-skilled domains of employment and entrepreneurship (Saxenian 1999). While the corporate world has continuously pressed national government to relax quotas on labor immigration, pleading a shortage of IT labor, upward wage pressure, and the need to maintain competitive advantage (Gleckman 1998; Moschella 1998), others fear that immigration will take high-tech jobs away from native-born Americans and lower their wages (Archey and Matloff 1998; Matloff 1995; Matloff 1996).

The story of a quota imposed by Congress in 1991 illustrates the practical consequences of these debates. As part of a larger scheme to stem the flow of immigrants, the quota allowed only 65,000 temporary workers to enter the country annually on H1-B visas, most of which go to programmers.[6] In 1997 the limit of 65,000 was reached before the end of the year, triggering a divisive debate in 1998—under the pressure of an increased demand for high-skilled IT labor in a booming information economy—about whether the limit should be raised. The intensity of the debate is reflected in various bills that were introduced, defeated, revived, passed, and rewritten through the efforts of the House of Representatives, the Senate, and the White House. The bill finally enacted, the American Competitiveness and Workforce Improvement Act of 1998, allowed 115,000 foreign workers to be granted visas for fiscal years 1999 and 2000; the number of visas was to drop slightly in 2001 and then revert to 65,000 in 2002. The bill also required employers to pay a new H-1B worker fee of $500 to fund training and educational programs for American workers. The 115,000 visas allotted for fiscal year 2000 were however exhausted in March 2000, forcing Congress to pass another act (the American Competitiveness in the Twenty-First Century Act of 2000) that increased the annual number of H-1B visas to 195,000 for the next three years. Under the new act, employers were required to pay a $1,000 fee for each H-1B application, with the fees used to generate $150 million a year in scholarships for American students. The act also required that the U.S. Immigration and Naturalization Service (INS), renamed the Bureau of Citizenship and Immigration Services (BCIS), not count someone toward the cap if that person had had H-1B status in the prior six years, unless he or she was authorized for a new six-year period of stay. The debates on the future of immigrant high-tech labor need to be reformulated, as I attempt to make visible the inefficacy of border enforcement against online IT labor flows (i.e., virtual migration). Using high-speed data communication links, programmers based in their national territories can work on line and in real time on computers situated anywhere in the world, thus obviating the process of material migration for both labor and corporations.

I do not suggest that territory-based integration will disappear because of the sheer force and supremacy of virtual techniques, nor do I think that one is a complete replacement for the other. My intent is to illuminate a complex field of transnational governance in which contemporary capitalism and modern nation-states may be undergoing actual and possible transformation. In the next few chapters, my aim is to interrogate as concretely and as specifically as possible how the constant revolution in the instruments of production, distribution, communication, and governance necessitates a rethinking of the existing institutional setup of states, corporate management, and the global workforce. By focusing on specific techniques of labor integration across national spaces, I also intend to make visible new vulnerabilities in social life. Just as digitized financial integration makes national economies—and thus their people—vulnerable to the transnational interests of capital, the digitized integration of labor makes labor markets and workers susceptible to pressures emanating from outside their national borders.

CHAPTER 3

Body Shopping

"Keep, ancient lands, your storied pomp!" cries she
With silent lips, "Give me your tired, your poor,
Your huddled masses yearning to breathe free,
The wretched refuse of your teeming shore.
Send these, the homeless, tempest-tost, to me,
I lift my lamp beside the golden door!"

—Emma Lazarus, "The New Colossus" (1883),

poem at the base of the Statue of Liberty

[The] master of any vessel who shall knowingly bring within the United
States on such vessel, and land or permit to be landed, any Chinese
laborer, from any foreign port of place, shall be deemed guilty of a mis-
demeanor, and on conviction thereof shall be punished by a fine of not
more than five hundred dollars for each and every such Chinese laborer
so brought, and may be also imprisoned for a term not exceeding one
year.—Chinese Exclusion Act of 1882

These two quotations, from the same period, may be read as highlight-
ing the gap or contrast between the ideal and the real. They may even
be read in terms of the contrast between race-free and race-based politics of
immigration. Both readings would be correct. But I stress a different incom-
patibility: free and open immigration versus immigration as a planned and
programmed event. The Chinese Exclusion Act of 1882 and the more general
Immigration Act of 1882 were both designed to prevent immigrant workers
from entering an American labor market hit by a general economic downturn in the 1870s. Widespread racism offered an easy criterion for exercising
economic closure. By contrast, the immigrant restrictions of 1882 were pre-
ceded by laws encouraging immigration from 1864 to 1868 to overcome the
reduced labor supply occasioned by the Civil War. The Chinese Exclusion

Act was finally repealed in 1943, the year when the labor-hungry war economy also saw the creation of the *bracero* program, under which a few million braceros—Mexican farm workers who performed seasonal contract labor—came to work the fields of the United States.

Migration research has long stressed the systemic causes and functions of immigrant labor for advanced industrial economies (Burawoy 1976; Castells 1975; Pedraza-Bailey 1990; Portes 1978) through the articulation of an international system (Portes and Böröcz 1989). Substantial but temporary increases in H-1B work visa permits by the U.S. Congress in the 1990s and 2000–01, in addition and perhaps in response to these structural forces, reflect an important tendency in American immigration policy: flexibility. To program a flexible opening or shut down immigration passages in response to the labor requirements of different business cycles has been a vital aspect of this policy. James Cockcroft (1986) aptly calls this a "revolving door" immigration policy, characterized by cycles of labor immigration and deportation. Whether it was the recruitment of Mexican immigrant workers by the Cotton Growers Association during the First World War and their subsequent deportation in 1920–22, or the creation of the bracero program, or the contemporary case of "cerebreros," the term used by Alarcón (2000) for immigrant programming labor since the cold war, immigration has been a field of deliberate intervention under the systemic imperatives of the American economy. It is no surprise that in times of economic downturn immigrants are seen as a "fiscal drain" (Calavita 1996) and tend to arouse anti-immigrant sentiments (Cornelius 1982; Espenshade and Calhoun 1992; Higham 1988). That the Bureau of Immigration was part of the Department of Commerce and Labor in the early twentieth century also shows that immigration was primarily a labor issue. Even when the Second World War prompted the transfer of the Immigration and Naturalization Service to the Department of Justice (Kurian and Harahan 1998), labor continued to be an important aspect of immigration policy, as shown by the bracero program and other initiatives. In the late 1990s, with an economic boom triggered mainly by the technology sector, the immigration door swung open again when the United States issued an unusually high number of work visas to high-tech labor. Computer-related and engineering occupations have consistently accounted for over 50 percent of H-1B petitions (appendix B, table 3), and in a recent count of employers who hired H-1B workers, the top twenty-five were all technology firms, including five Indian subsidiaries (see appendix B, table 1). Clearly, the importance of cerebreros for the new information and network-based economy could not be overstated.

In the global competition for programming labor, the flexibility of American immigration policy has even inspired countries such as Germany that have historically been less open to labor immigration. In 2000 Germany introduced a short-term visa program—oddly termed the Green Card initiative[1]—to attract high-skilled programming labor, with seemingly tempting offers such as a five-year work permit for those with a college degree in information technology, permission to bring families, whose members could also work, and permission to change jobs within the five-year period (Greenfield 2000). Still, Germany remains at a competitive disadvantage: "The assumption that Germany is very attractive for top IT experts from India is probably not very realistic," said Hartmut Schwesinger, the executive director of Frankfurt's economic development agency ("Indian IT Pros" 2000). The United States—with higher wages and the use of English—is a favorite destination of Indian high-tech workers, who account for the majority of all high-tech workers brought to the United States from overseas: "nearly half of the H-1B petitions were granted to persons born in India, which far exceeded China, the next leading country . . . [and] nearly 74% of the systems analysts and programmers were born in India compared to about 18% in all other occupations," according to government estimates (Immigration and Naturalization Service 2000; see Appendix B, table 2).[2]

The mechanism by which systems analysts and programmers from India come to the United States on H-1B visas is generally called *body shopping*. Consultancy firms shop for skilled bodies—i.e., recruit software professionals—in India to contract them out for short-term projects in the United States. At the end of the projects, programmers look for other projects, usually through the same contractors. Most employers in the United States find this mode of recruitment convenient since it saves them time, money, and employment obligations. "Body shopping is essentially when people are sitting in some kind of recruitment shops in India," a spokesperson for a national association of software industry in New Delhi explained. "They're really sending out our talented people . . . they do not enter into any kind of service contract but only into contract for providing people on a temporary basis. So while those people continue to work for their local company, they're deploying their services for an overseas customer, for a foreign customer on site." A consultant who was himself recruited through body shopping further explained, "You can say, these are like headhunters . . . What they can do is they can get you an interview for all these big companies, if they need a full-time employee they can place you there."

Body shopping carries a slightly negative connotation. Companies in India that do not engage in body shopping tend to deny having anything to do with it; they also consider it an inferior, though lucrative, business practice. They emphasize that they provide real services (like developing complete software systems for various clients) and carefully avoid the "sham" of merely placing software professionals with needy corporations in the United States. They equate the programming labor used in body shopping with alteration work done by tailors: "you have a shirt already developed, and now there is a cut; you give it to the alteration guy and ask, can you [fix] it for me?" Although almost all the big software firms in India could become big only through body shopping (including many of the subsidiaries listed in appendix B), there is a certain shame in not being in the business of marketable products. Therefore the companies that do engage in body shopping couch the practice in euphemisms such as "consultancy." A few people who came to the United States as consultants did take pride in their work: "As a consultant you need to know more than [the company's regular] employees," a programmer claimed.

More important than the image of firms and software professionals is how body shopping—as a practice of labor recruitment and labor control—is in itself a remarkable phenomenon. I identify four important characteristics after a careful analysis of body shopping. While the first two highlight the *character* of programming labor, the last two illuminate the *method* of employment through body shopping. In the sections that follow, I explore each of these characteristics: (1) universal as opposed to specific labor; (2) systems-level labor; (3) higher-earning but low-cost labor; (4) just-in-time labor.

Universal as Opposed to Specific Labor

One important characteristic of programming labor in general is its relative universality.[3] Unlike some forms of labor that are applicable only to one sector of the economy (such as a surgeon's or a civil engineer's), the work done by software professionals is needed by many industries and directly affects the products or services that they provide. Thus even though a surgeon may be hired by an airline, the surgeon's work does not affect how the planes will be controlled or how the tickets will be issued. But programming labor by nature recodes in binary digits all possible types of tasks that earlier existed in different forms. Because of its capacity for universal coding, software can be developed not only for white-collar jobs such as ticketing but also for controlling heavy machines in industrial plants. The structuring of work as a general problem of coding also creates conditions for a new, increasingly universal medium of work across different jobs and occupations. Ubiquitous computer screens become the ground of work performance, with layers of software codes forming the new programmable schemes of work and its organization. Unlike other forms of labor that cater to specific occupations and industries, programming labor touches a vast number of occupations and unrelated industries. Programming increasingly provides the language of work in general (see chapter 5). I do not wish to suggest that programming is less than a specific activity, as it does consist of specific acts of writing code; I stress only its universal relevance to a variety of organizations and work situations.

In an important sense, we live in a programmed and programmable world. Acts of programming inform and define the world of automated teller machines, geographical positioning systems, personal digital assistants, microwaves, digital video, word processing, databases, global capital flows, and the Internet. Perhaps the term "information age" is not specific enough to describe this world. After all, newspapers, magazines, books, radio, and television also belong to the world of information and its dissemination. A more precise description of our age must focus on programming and Boolean logic, now installed in the cars one drives, the computers one uses, the video games one plays, and the smart bombs that the state drops. It is no mere accident that software professionals lend their labor and expertise to an unprecedented diversity of businesses. Triggered by programming, most organizations are undergoing major changes, prompting a phenomenal growth of body-shopping firms. "[Body-shopping firms] are all over the place and they're making a lot of money," as a programmer put it. In light of the universal application of their work, I noticed during field research that Indian programmers were being quickly deployed, transferred, and redeployed in industries as diverse as aviation, financial services, health care, insurance, pharmaceuticals, technology, shipping, apparel, animation, accounting, Internet services, and even the U.S. military. This need for programmers in such a variety of enterprises highlights the ability of programming to develop new schemes of organizational governance connecting everyone as nodes in networks with different architectural designs (see the discussion of "algocratic governance" in chapter 5).

Systems-Level Labor

The universality of programming is not like the universality of secretarial work in diverse organizations. Unlike secretaries, software professionals are systems-level workers who can potentially transform how organizations function from within. As programmers, they not only help translate the previous work set-up into a digital format, as when they convert a face-to-face banking system into an online one, they also help to transform—in their capacity as systems analysts—some fundamental aspects of how an organization functions, as when they reconfigure various departments and hierarchies through software schemes like Enterprise Resource Planning (ERP) systems. Using such systems, software professionals can be asked to chalk out a new work flow, using optimal networking to transform the dynamics of the supplier-business-customer chain, identifying redundancies, and mechanizing the work process from the designing stage to the shop floor, implementing a software-based, universal medium of work.

The pervasive medium of electronic texts and graphics is not neutral to what gets performed through it; rather, in the "medium is the message" sense of Marshall McLuhan (1994), it helps to constitute work in specific ways. Consequently, many previous methods of doing work have become redundant, and are in the process of being abolished and replaced by less differentiated forms of work performance. The following description of the heterogeneity and division of work prevailing in the 1950s, described by C. Wright Mills, is in need of a revision: "In the enormous file of the office, in all the calculating rooms, accountants and purchasing agents replace the man who did his own figuring. And in the lower reaches of the white-collar world, office operatives grind along, loading and emptying the filing system; there are private secretaries and typists, entry clerks, billing clerks, corresponding clerks—a thousand kinds of clerks; the operators of light machinery, comptometers, Dictaphones, addressographs; and the receptionists to let you in or keep you out" (Mills 1951, x).

As programmers introduce advanced information systems at the workplace, "a thousand kinds of clerks" are giving way to delayered and flatter organizational structures. This change in the very *organization* of organizations is a phenomenon viewed both positively because of its implications for lean, decentralized, "post-bureaucratic" management (Hirschhorn 1984; Kanter 1991; Piore 1996) and negatively because of the displacements and temporization resulting from the structural transformation of work (Aronowitz and DiFazio 1994; Callaghan and Hartmann 1991; Doeringer 1991). With a widespread demand for programming labor in different organizations, software professionals are well-paid workers. However, the practice of shopping for cheaper bodies at the global level and the methods of their employment lower the cost of programmers and systems analysts in the United States.

High-Earning but Low-Cost Labor

Software professionals who temporarily migrate from India to work in the United States are both expensive and cheap for American corporations to hire. The seeming paradox of higher-earning but lower-cost labor is easy to understand. Although contract workers, placed with different companies by their parent body-shopping firms, may be earning high salaries in the short term because their high-level skills are in short supply,[4] in the long term they are still low-cost labor. Annual contracts may fetch high incomes for these temporary workers, at times higher than the annual salaries of regular employees in similar positions. But they also allow the receiving company to trim its workforce, take these temporary workers into service only in times of need, and economize on long-term benefits—social security, retirement contributions, health insurance, and unemployment insurance—that must be provided to permanent employees. "Actually it's a win-win situation for me and the company," said a programmer, "What happens is that [my company][5] doesn't have to hire [a permanent] employee. They don't have to pay for my insurance. And they can fire me. I'm not a liability for them. But in [re]turn they have to pay more money. So if I worked full-time, I would probably get half the amount . . . the other thing is if they hired a full-time employee they would have to [spend money in order to] train him."

I heard a few conflicting stories about the earnings of contract versus permanent workers. Many contract workers think they earn more than what the regular employees of the company receive. "If I worked [for this company as a permanent employee]," a contract programmer said, "I would get .6 or .7 of what I get now. I think so. But who knows, I don't go out and ask people. That's the general idea." But the question "Who earns more?" does not have a stable answer. First, the body-shopping or consultancy firm pockets almost one-third to two-thirds of the consultant's salary. Second, a programmer arriving directly from India definitely earns less than the person who has spent some time in the United States or graduated from an American university. When you come from India "you would convert the dollars into rupees and it seems like a huge amount to you," a programmer ruminated, "but after a year or two, you just catch up. It's just the initial couple of years that you see a huge difference but then it starts shrinking. Then it depends how good you are."

Perhaps we should differentiate between two situations relating to contract labor. The first involves programmers who remain employees of their recruiting company in India, and are only technically employed with their client in the United States—they merely receive a maintenance allowance in the United States, paid by their mother company in India. The total cost to the American firm in this case is many times less than the cost of employing an equivalent American worker. In the second situation, however, these same professionals, once they are in the United States and gain experience, start looking for a contractor based in the United States and attempt to secure a more lucrative placement. As the vice-president of a software firm based in New Delhi confessed, four of his six employees did not return to India after completing their projects in the United States. Consultants must be good at negotiating with their employers to earn more. "Let's say I get $70," a programmer explains, "but with my background, I say I need to move on; then they ask how much I want, and I say $100 per hour, and they will say okay. They will find out . . . if [another company] can increase your salary . . . they will say this guy is useful here, he has done a commendable job, let's make a deal . . . So if I said $100, they might say okay they have got something for $90 . . . So if you go for an interview you can find out where you stand."

The biggest advantage of hiring contract labor is not low short-term costs; it is flexibility, and the resulting reduction of the long-term costs of maintaining a large permanent workforce. A systems analyst admitted that consultants must work harder and be technically more "savvy" to survive, because "tomorrow they [may] shelve this plan, shelve credit risk management, and that the consultants go first." Body shopping is a highly flexible postindustrial labor practice. Because they provide a universal kind of labor, software workers find themselves, more than other subcontracted workers, operating within a flexible regime of just-in-time labor.

Just-in-Time Labor

One sunny afternoon I drove to Princeton, New Jersey, to meet five consultants—all males, perhaps twenty-four to thirty years old. All were sharing a modest, sparsely furnished, relatively new suburban house. The house seemed a bit dark, empty and silent despite the crowd of six in the same room. The conversation, awkward to begin with, soon began to fade. One consultant kept watching television while I was trying to tape-record the conversation. As a stubborn researcher, I stayed there for an hour despite the noticeably estranged, uninvolved, and hesitant voices of the consultants. The interview expectedly failed to provide any new insights. Later, I was told that the consultants whom I had just met were living in a house rented by their parent company for programmers who were between projects or who had recently arrived from India and were still waiting to receive their first assignment. A picture began to emerge—all the consultants that afternoon were part of a reserve army of programming labor to be deployed just in time as soon as a demand was noticed in an organization. Perhaps being out of projects was a demoralizing experience for some of them, and not the right time for the researcher to visit them.

Body shopping demonstrates with extraordinary clarity what "flexible" forms of postindustrial labor mean and entail. This form of labor is analogous to the application of the just-in-time (JIT) techniques developed by several Japanese firms in the 1970s for inventory management. This new system drastically reduced large inventories and associated overhead costs throughout the entire production system by relying on the careful scheduling of a precise delivery of parts and supplies in small amounts, made by vendors just in time. Just like a large inventory, a large, permanent workforce maintained with no regard to the seasonal highs and lows of a business is a costly problem which the practice of body shopping attempts to overcome in its own way. By programming the supply of software professionals accurately and only for the length of time needed, body-shopping firms help various companies to reduce this cost. "If a new project comes up and you need ten people tomorrow, they will provide you ten people. It's amazing, these guys are so professional," a software professional based in the United States explained.

The just-in-time system of labor poses an obvious question. What do programmers do when they are "on the bench," that is, when they have just arrived from India but have not got their first assignment, or when they are between projects, waiting to be deployed just in time at the next client site? Who pays for this unneeded reserve labor inventory with all its overhead costs? The body-shopping firm must decide how much to pay consultants during these periods in accordance with its bench policy. Typically, in 1999–2000 a newly arrived programmer received a monthly stipend of only $1,000 before going to work on his or her first project. During subsequent bench periods, consulting companies were required by law to pay the consultant's full salary. Yet many body-shopping firms—which hired professionals in anticipation of a surge in demand—ended up transferring the financial burden to the consultant by cutting pay as much as 75 percent from the original level.

Thus, the flexibility of a system based on just-in-time labor relies in large part on the immense flexibility demanded from workers themselves, entailing a shift of responsibility from the system to the worker. *Silicon India*, a monthly technology and business magazine, conveys the corporate demand of worker responsibility very clearly: "people often have the misconception that consulting companies must mind the careers of their consultants. But in fact, the onus of career management is on the consultant himself" (Anand 2001). A flexible system of just-in-time labor is not viable in itself without making the worker bear the burden in cases of failure. A worker must also be flexible enough to keep learning new skills, especially in the realm of software, where a plethora of technologies—Weblogic, JavaBeans, MQ series, C++, Visual Basic, DB2, IMS, and Oracle—seem to emerge continually. Obviously the bench period is the best time to upgrade one's skills: "use this time to learn new and marketable skills," *Silicon India* advises. "Don't depend on anyone else to find your work—go look for a new job on your own, you must be 'resume ready' and prepared for the next job at all times . . . as a contractor, one should never have the illusion of job security—you have to keep moving and marketing yourself even before your current project is over" (Anand 2001, 52). The advice also assumes that workers will show a certain amount of transnational flexibility: "Surprising as this may seem, return home for a while, chill, get married, get trained in a new technology or travel. Wait outside the U.S. for a year and get a new six-year lease for your H-1B visa. Take a job in Europe, Singapore, Australia, the UK or the Gulf for a year or two" (Anand 2001). The economic downturn of the United States in 2001, coupled with the flexible system of layoffs, made the system of just-in-time programming labor even more precarious for workers.

Flexibility and Its Discontents

The need for systemic as well as production flexibility is not a new phenomenon. Flexibility has been an issue of great discussion for production and employment, viewed both negatively (Harvey 1989) and positively (Piore and Sabel 1984). Following Jürgen Habermas (1988), we can understand the flexibility achieved at the cost of the worker in terms of an internal colonization of the lifeworld by the system. Society, according to Habermas, is at once a *lifeworld* and a *system*.[6] From the lifeworld perspective, we may conceptualize society as primarily a symbolically structured space of social interaction, understanding, and experience. Our lifeworld—comprising both private and public spheres—acts as the ground of what is said, discussed, or addressed in a situation among friends, family, acquaintances, and strangers in homes, restaurants, offices, and public forums. More specifically, the lifeworld consists of cultural space, social space, and personality space, responsible for three processes of reproduction: cultural reproduction, social integration, and socialization. "In coming to an understanding with one another about their situation, participants in communication stand in a cultural tradition which they use and at the same time renew" (Habermas 1988, 137). In addition to the symbolic reproduction of culture, communicative action also helps to coordinate action, serving *social integration* and social solidarity. "Finally, under the aspect of *socialization*, communicative action serves the formation of personal identities" (Habermas 1988, 137).[7] In addition to conceptualizing society as the lifeworld in which actions are coordinated through harmonizing *action orientations* leading to social integration, Habermas also conceives of society as a self-regulating *system* in which actions are coordinated through functional interconnections of *action consequences*, resulting in greater system integration. In capitalist societies, for example, the market is one of those systemic mechanisms that coordinate actions by action consequences that penalize or reward certain kinds of behavior. The goal-directed, profit-seeking behavior of a company manager is not just a result of socialization and cultural values (lifeworld); it is also the functional requirement of a competitively structured field of capitalism, in which nonprofit orientation is rendered unviable, driven out of circulation by its action consequences. Although higher levels of system complexity enhance society's capacity to steer itself for material reproduction and survival, they may also lead—as they have in the modern world—to the "colonization of the lifeworld by the system" (Habermas 1988) as the lifeworld structures responsible for social integration are increasingly subordinated to the system imperatives of functional integration. The notion of just-in-time labor exemplifies to a degree the colonization of the lifeworld for systemic purposes. While the flexibility of loading and unloading workers does help the economic system to achieve greater efficiency, it is at the same time disruptive of the lifeworld, which is harnessed more and more toward system imperatives.

Economic sociologists may question the separation of system and lifeworld. Isn't the system embedded in networks of social relations, and thus the lifeworld, in the first place? Isn't the whole idea of system as independent of social relations a mere thought experiment at best, and a grievous misunderstanding at worst? For economic sociologists, the market as a systemic mechanism free from the lifeworld, which it colonizes with its "invisible hand," would be a misconception. "The anonymous market of neoclassical models," Granovetter (1985) argues, "is virtually non-existent in economic life." Markets can take place only within the dense social networks and culturally shared meanings that sustain them. The market for venture capital in

Silicon Valley is a good example of the importance of social networks (Dossani and Kumar 2005).

Habermas anticipates and accommodates much of economic sociology and its criticism of economic theory. He agrees that all formal systemic mechanisms of the market or bureaucracies are always anchored in the social. All interactions are still connected through the mechanism of mutual understanding and trust. In the absence of what Durkheim called "noncontractual elements of a contract," no business could be conducted. If such communicative interactions were banished from formal structures, no organizational goals would be achieved. After all, the separation of the system and the lifeworld is only analytical, and although one could connect actual institutions with each perspective—like market with system, and family with lifeworld—Habermas cautions against such crude identifications. Nevertheless, he agrees with the classical model of bureaucracy or the economic models of the market at least in one respect—the relative neutralization of lifeworld perspective. "Action within organization falls *under the premise* of formally regulated domains of action. Because the latter are ethically neutralized by their legal form of organization, *communicative action forfeits its validity basis in the interior of organizations*" (Habermas 1988, 310). Let us recall, for instance, M. G. Garcia's analysis (via Callon 1999) of the transformation in France of the table strawberry market into a computerized market, which by design disconnected buyers and sellers from one another. While buyers and sellers knew each other personally in the earlier system, and thus displayed less calculative behavior, under the new system they became calculating, atomistic individuals who came together only for market transactions. At all times, quantity supplied and quantity demanded were evident to all buyers and sellers, and a bidding system ensured that an equilibrium price resulted. With the tools of computerized displays, constantly updated prices and quantities, and the ability to compare directly the quality of one basket to another, the market participants became the calculating agents whom most economists assume them to be. Economic theory's assumptions and assertions about human nature did not describe an existing *homo economicus* who was discovered in a strawberry market in France. Instead, the deliberate performance of largely invalid assumptions about human behavior in this market created a reality that conveniently made the theory's predictions appear to be accurate. That this occurred also demonstrates a concrete instance of the internal colonization of the lifeworld by the system. Members of social networks in market or bureaucratic institutions trust and communicate with each other *with two qualifications*: first, the formal basis of institutions becomes the ground of legitimation, disempowering communicative action, which loses the ability to invoke outside norms and values decisively (e.g., a profit-making enterprise rules out a nonprofit orientation); second, participants become primarily interested in the consequences of their actions, orienting themselves to "values" in a purposive-rational manner, and thus adopt an objectifying attitude to each other, transforming social and intrapsychic relations into instrumental relations.

In fact, we can stretch Habermas's thesis of internal colonization to such an extent that structures of lifeworld may appear fully assimilated to the system and it may not be possible to talk about them as standing apart in any real sense. While discussing tendencies toward juridification, Habermas himself argues that to alleviate the class conflict lodged in the sphere of production, the welfare state must provide social services and thus perform the juridification of lifeworld, spreading "a net of client relationships over private spheres of life" through social services, schools, and family law. As a result of capitalist growth, the subsystems of economy and state become more and more complex, penetrating ever deeper into the symbolic reproduction of the lifeworld:

> The trend toward juridification . . . is gaining ground along a broad front—the more leisure, culture, recreation, and tourism recognizably come into the grip of the laws of the commodity economy and the definitions of mass consumption, the more the structure of bourgeois family manifestly become adapted to the imperatives of the employment system, the more school palpably takes over the functions of assigning job and life prospects, and so forth . . . Juridification means, in the first place, the establishment of basic legal principles: recognition of the child's fundamental rights against his parents, of the wife's against her husband, of the pupil's against the school . . . While the core areas of family law (governing marriage, support, matrimonial property, divorce, parental care, guardianship) have been reformed via adjudication (i.e., court decisions) and via legislation . . . (Habermas 1988, 368)

Perhaps the assimilation of the lifeworld into the system goes beyond juridification. If later communicative practices depend on children's primary socialization, such system-driven media as television ensure that the very basis of the lifeworld—norms, values, and linguistic frameworks—are mediated by system imperatives. It is not merely a question of early consumerist values and cradle-to-grave brand loyalty consciously inculcated among the young through more than $15 billion spent on marketing to children in the United States every year; it is also a subtler issue of identity and individualized ethic. Schools further help to produce competitive students fit for the competitive economy. In an individualized examination system, students receive a good or bad grade and feel euphoric or anxious; they also experience a fundamental isolation from all others. In this context, how do we think about the lifeworld in terms of spontaneous opinion formation, will formation, or undistorted communication, standing apart from the system? It seems that the system is self-validating: it produces, as Hardt and Negri (2000) argue, its own legitimation by rendering ineffective any contradiction in social fabrics. If the system increasingly makes available possible spaces for negotiation, and possible forms of the lifeworld including discourses of productivity, efficiency, and control, it is difficult to think of the lifeworld as being outside the system except as an impossible ideal. However, I want to be a little cautious about characterizing the system as an all-encompassing, unitary machine, leading us down a single path. I would regard the system as a bundle of programming schemes, which being plural in character contain the always present possibility of contradictions and indeterminacy.

Before you forget what this chapter was about, I should discuss how body-shopping firms—being part of a transnational, capitalistic system of labor supply—use certain schemes of recruitment to incite specific desires among Indian programmers. In this rendering of the lifeworld, the lives of programmers display curious transnational affinities as they swing between nations and between fantasy and despair.

Transnational Affinities:
Between Fantasy and Despair

In seeking to recruit programming labor, body-shopping firms incite fantasies of the West, tapping into desires produced by the earlier colonial system as well as an almost innate fascination with the unknown, the uncharted, and the unfamiliar (along with the fear of the unknown). An image of the

Text within the advertisement:

FIGURE 1. *Fantasy as a recruitment strategy.*

Empire State Building in New York that appeared in an ad in the Indian technology magazine *Dataquest* (figure 1) illustrates how body-shopping firms arouse fantasy as a recruitment strategy.

In the advertisement a man in professional attire, shown in silhouette, looks longingly from afar at the New York skyline bathed in an evening glow. The caption reads: "At HCL-Perot, your skills can take you a long, long way." Other advertisements are similar.

While tempting offers of international placements are common in Indian newspapers and magazines, the fantasies thus aroused are not necessarily false. American society is undeniably affluent. As one software professional in New Delhi put it: "It is hard to let go of swanky cars," and many others similarly talked about the physical conditions of American life. When imagined from India, life in the United States emerges as a series of scenes from Hollywood films and television: beautiful beaches and bodies, fast cars, a mesmerizing use of technology in everyday life, and breathtaking visual stimulation through glittering shops and malls. When these programmers get a chance to visit the United States to work on projects, this fantasy becomes for a while a lived fantasy. It does not disappear all of a sudden, as parts of the fantasy do correspond with reality. These programmers are able to buy cars that were overpriced or unavailable in India and experience the visual stimulation of the malls and beaches, all the while working for the most part in coastal cities of the United States. The role of technologies behind these lived fantasies is important.

As trained technology workers, the programmers frankly acknowledge the significance of technologies in their choices: "If I were [in India], I wouldn't have got exposed to so much technology . . . I would have never thought of buying a computer for home [in India] . . . So you could be smart but if you're not exposed to all these technologies, you can never grow. And that's the big advantage here. Because I know, my father still doesn't have access to e-mail. And when I go to India, to these Internet shops, you can't even get a [phone] line to connect; getting a connection is very difficult. So, you miss all these technologies."

Gradually the fantasy recedes and other aspects of reality appear, including experiences of cultural alienation. Desires for attractive bodies stay elusive and unmet. Programmers come to know a populace struggling against obesity, consuming antidepressants, and experiencing loneliness and homelessness, the reality of which was absent in earlier seductions and fantasies. The most devastating realization is one of political and social exclusion, of being constituted as the "other." This realization is particularly difficult because the programmers come from respected middle-class families in India and are a high-earning group even in the United States.

As the transnational economic system brings different lifeworlds together, programmers now negotiate the combined effects of two forms of total closure. In its institutionalized form, total closure sets in place state bureaucratic mechanisms that control the practice of body shopping under nationalist concerns about immigration, constituting the programmers as "aliens," whereas in its non-institutionalized or cognitive form total closure speaks through the nationalist self-identification of transnational workers, who despite unsteady identities recognize themselves as Indians alone. This nation-based closure creates a sense of exclusion among the programmers living in the United States: they are made to feel both explicitly and implicitly critical of the United States (and induced to fantasize about their life in India) without being aware of the forces of nation-based closure that structure their life. This critical stance is expressed by them in many ways: "In the U.S., you are always a second-class, second-grade citizen. There will always be one incident daily or once in a month or once in six months to remind you that you are not part of them, that you are not an American."

Physical appearance also plays a major part in this feeling of exclusion. One systems analyst explained, "I have this identity as a Sikh. Going around in the malls you can always see in their faces. What's that, the funny cap you have? Or 'I like your cap.'" The discourse of race also enters into the programmers' consciousness, who grapple with "whiteness" as the dominant self-image of nationality in the imaginary social space of the United States. Most Indians become highly conscious of not passing that test, especially if their own nationalistic gaze as well as the gaze of those around them finds them deviating from white normality. A project manager who returned to India despite good chances of finding a permanent employer in the United States complained about seeing opportunities of promotion limited by racial closures: "Again in the long-term, it's questionable whether they will allow you to rise above a certain level. As you see the top-level of management is always white Caucasian male . . . Wherever I have worked in the U.S., even in Japan [where] I used to work for Citibank, which is a U.S. company, even there the top management was always white Caucasian male. Not even women, not even blacks." Some immigrant professionals blame widespread prejudice in the United States: "They are just prejudiced. Definitely. They may not actually be fully conscious, or it's very subtle. It might not be evident directly; they might say we are an equal opportunity people." Perhaps this perceived prejudice was less about felt discrimination and more about a glass ceiling. Although workers from India received a disproportionately small number of top managerial positions, they did not complain of any direct racial tension, which may be more visible on the streets than in the workplaces: "Not that you feel any racial tension in your work environment. But it's just on the roads, shopping malls. [People] can be prejudiced. They're not educated, they can say anything, they're not so broad-minded.

That's all. I mean people who you interact with on the road. The people you work with, the people you deal with professionally . . . definitely there is no problem."

The realization of being the "other"—along with the struggle against cultural difference stemming from a different language of togetherness in the form of altered expectations and sociality in the United States—gives rise to general despair and disappointment. Programmers become highly aware that different languages are used in India and the United States to describe togetherness and how one relates to others. In the United States, in all friendships and family ties there is a tendency to avoid taking the other for granted, for reasons related to freedom, privacy, and closures of individual sovereignty. In India, on the other hand, a taken-for-grantedness defines friendships and family ties, differentiating them from mere acquaintances and formal relationships. One of my informants was struck that in the United States one is expected to call friends before dropping by. "Even if I go to my friend's place," he said, "I have to call and say I'm coming, like an appointment. You know what I mean. I couldn't just walk into my friend's place, [which] means I am intruding upon their privacy . . . it's like, were we expecting you here? You could be friends for six years, but you couldn't do it. Just walk in." This immigrant experience extends to the workplace. In India, the boundary between a friend and colleague tends to blur with increased interaction. "When you work here, you don't really get to know anybody," a female software professional explained, "In India when you have worked, even for, let's say, two months, you are totally free with each other, you know each other very well, you go to each other's houses, and start getting together. That doesn't happen here . . . Coming from India, you get used to that kind of stuff. I just think that a place where everything is just professional, though people are very nice and helpful, you don't really develop that kind of bond that you do in India." This bond is nothing but the taken-for-grantedness assumed in most friendships in India. The discontent emanating from a specific immigrant condition finds expression in a variety of forms. It is not surprising that programmers do not intend to stay permanently in the United States. They put forward a variety of reasons to go back to India:

"It feels more safe in India than here . . ."

"I miss family ties. My niece keeps growing and I can't even see her . . ."

"If I'm sick, I can always depend on my neighbors in India . . ."

"I belong to India. That's my country . . ."

The vast and rich literature on diasporas, and South Asian diasporas in particular, has highlighted experiences of displacement, resettlement, and the invention of identities and homeland traditions along new social frameworks that make diasporas visible (Cohen 1997; Kumar 2000; Leonard 1992; Myers 1998; Prashad 2000; Sivanandan 1982). The role of capital in migratory dislocations, both historical (Kale 1998) and current (Sassen 1998), is also important. It would be hard to deny the effects of a restrictive labor regime—body shopping—on programmers' attitudes. The economics of body shopping—its temporary and flexible approach to work—produce unsettling effects in programmers' lives.

Even though programmers are determined to go back to India, their critical attitude toward the United States largely disappears once they have done so, and they invariably look forward to coming back to the United States for another stint. Nostalgia for the other nation is at the heart of the transnational immigrant condition, and this is something that goes beyond simple nationalism. Lacking a transnational or postnationalist mode of apprehending reality, the programmers continually long for the "other" nation: they miss India while in the United States and miss the United States when they are back in India. One's situation in the transnational economic system may perhaps be characterized as one of chronic national misplacement. "When you're there you want to be here, and when you are here you want to be there," a programmer explained in a moment of reflection, "When you are here, you start missing home a lot. Because here, life is totally different. Right? I don't know my neighbors here. In India, as soon as I go back, the neighbors come to my room and say hello. So it's like two different places. When you're here you miss that life, when you're there you miss this life. Here, it's like I can just take my car and go anywhere I want to go. It's totally like two extreme zones."

Some of the programmers were well aware of this immigrant situation and of their failed attempts to fit in wherever they were. One programmer talked about how cultural distance remained a barrier despite conscious efforts to expand his social self, to include strange others of a different world: "The problem is that most of the people, even Indians who come here, they try to change, you try to go with this culture . . . but [one is] never able to get into this culture." Taking roots in new cultural soil is never easy. Although competence in English or programming languages may be a requirement adequate for employment, it falls short of the greater objective of living a life full of meaning. Programmers, perhaps like every other immigrant category, miss connections, culture, and community: "All the connections," as one programmer said. "Two different worlds . . . You kind of miss all those ties here [in the United States]. Like I'd know my parents are there and I end up calling them every week. You miss all that, family issues." When these migrants — the hobos of an integrated world — go back to India, one would like to assume that their life is restored to its harmony, that the earth is regained under the feet. But their reincarnation as transnational creatures precludes any return to the settled contentment of earlier life. There is not much solace within national enclosures for transnationally stirred souls. Memories of the good life in the United States haunt all who return to India: "You get spoiled by all the comfort that you have here [in the United States]. Because also, here it's a consumer market; in India it doesn't work that way. Here if I don't get anything . . . if the phone bill is wrong, I'm so used to calling them, saying I'm not paying for this, I didn't make this call. But in India, this thing doesn't work. You just have to pay for it; otherwise, you know what I mean. So, once you go there, you start missing this kind of stuff. Oh my God it was so easy to get it there, like planning a vacation, I could just go on vacation . . . everything is there, you and rental cars, you don't have to talk to anybody. Those comforts spoil you. Although you still think that you want to go back [to India], but once you go back you start missing all these things."

This is not to suggest that the structural and political position of the transnational programmer promotes a subjectivity more fraught or complex than any other. The point is to add more specificity to this particular mode of being — the transnational condition — produced within circuits of the economic system. Experiences of programmers belie several commonly held, though somewhat paradoxical, notions that immigrants lack an emotional attachment to the new place despite living and enjoying the fruits of the affluent society, or conversely, that that they never want go back and always look for permanent settlement in the United States. One can easily see how immigrant programmers miss being in the United States when they have left it, and look forward to coming back for another spell and renewing their attachment. One can also see that they wish to return to India during their stay in the United States. The transnational condition means that one loses a single cultural or national mode of being without being aware of it, that one is reborn without the memory of the past life; only those who saw the person before are struck by the change. One programmer captured this phenomenon in a remarkable moment of introspection: "The problem is, [when] you go back [to India], they just comment on you. You get mentally changed here too . . . the problem is when you go back, they think you have changed but you know you have not changed, [but have become] just so normal here [in the United States]."

This transformation of being-in-the-world is so subtle that one does not recognize it as change; it becomes a crucial part of one's perceptual lens. Not that previous subjectivity was fixed and static, only to be rewritten through migration experiences: in a way, all identities are hybrids. Recent works in cultural studies (Bhabha 1994; Hall 1996) have emphasized the concept of "hybridity" to underscore cultural fusions, ambiguities of identities, and "constructed" closures of race, nation, and ethnicity. Bhabha (1994) in particular examines the "liminal" or "interstitial" space "between" recognized traditions, finding the "location of culture" in the marginal, haunting, "unhomely" spaces between dominant social formations. Still, it is undeniable that subjectivities get constituted through dominant discursive practices. Experiences of migration stir up the settled and tranquil dust of subjectivity. Still bound up with the systemic frame of total closure, the resulting subjectivity tends to orient itself, in the case of programmers, to the other enclosure, the other nation. This forever elusive character of the transnational migrant condition is significant. It creates a consciousness that exists where it is not. It always seeks fulfillment in being elsewhere. As one systems analyst said, "When you're [in the United States] you want to go back, when you are there, you think you had a good life here." Even those who go back to India, with a permanent commitment to a single national space, tend to display transnational orientation without being aware of it. Many software executives who made a final decision to go back to India still maintained their U.S. permanent residency. One executive, who was "pretty happy" with his situation in India, said: "When I came back I thought I would go back [to the United States], but now I like it here [in India]." Yet in the same interview he said: "I have been traveling [to the United States] just once in six months, once in six months just to keep my Green Card current, but the need to travel has come down." This executive was managing an American subsidiary in India while maintaining direct communication links to a team in the United States—by e-mail, video conferencing, telephone, and intra-net—thus diminishing the need for work-related travel. Attempts to maintain permanent residency in the United States while residing permanently and resolutely in India are neither mere individual contradictions nor signs of simple opportunism. Individually, they are paradoxes produced by the desire to live a transnational life in a nation-based discursive frame. Institutionally, they reflect the conflicts of a transnational labor regime governed by a system of nation-states. Admittedly a true transnational order would not necessarily be preferable to an international one, as the problems of just-in-time labor and the harnessing and subordination of labor to dominant ends would still exist. But a transnational professional class has developed, one that takes after what Sklair (2001) calls a "transnational capitalistic class" with its own peculiar characteristics and orientation.

Dilemmas associated with the transnational condition may suggest that what the programmers desire from the United States is material, while what they derive from India is more social, emotional, and relational. The resulting subjectivity of individual programmers, one may suggest, balances between the pulls of materialism against social dispositions. Perhaps. But we also find high-level executives who enjoy material luxuries in India such as chauffeur-driven cars, plush houses, and domestic help at home and yet still try to maintain their permanent residency in the United States. Clearly there is something more than the mere material comforts of life that orients them to the United States even while they reside in India.

One may ask why there is no development of a more substantive, even if ambivalent, identity among the immigrants. The reason is simple. In conscious moments of identity, programmers were absolutely sure of their substantive identity; they understood and identified themselves as "Indian" with complete certainty. There was no uncertainty in that respect, and therefore no need for a new identity. Despite this self-understanding, determined partly by the discursive frame of total closure about their identity, their subjective orientation was not fixed or unambiguous in practice: it was constantly shaped and shifted by possibilities of life in other locations where they were not residing. One may also wonder why the programmers do not see their position in the United States as temporary in accordance with their immigration status, and why they miss the United States as the other home when they return to India. In fact, the programmers do know that their situation is not permanent, even if permanent residency status is always a possibility. They are not yet a transplanted community; they are temporary, yet transformed. They do develop local attachments, perhaps unconsciously, even while subjectively oriented toward the other nation. Even transplanted communities and permanent immigrants that tend to understand themselves in total categories such as "Indian" or "Korean," and presumably do not suffer from the second generation's anxiety about total identity definitions, hide from themselves their transnational orientation. The much discussed re-creation of homeland traditions serves the need for a familiar and comfortable milieu in a new place; it also has something to do with "being where one is not." One only needs to trace the return of immigrants back to India to see their efforts at re-creating a certain American ambiance at home.

In light of various schemes of global integration characterized by increased mass migrations and transnational cultural flows, some recent works have highlighted the unhinging of place and culture, examining how identities and subjectivities are themselves affected by mobility and displacement (Appadurai 1990; Gupta and Ferguson 1997). The story told here—of the transnational condition of Indian programmers who migrate to the United States temporarily or permanently—continues this line of thought. Specifically, what is important is how the complex subjectivities of transnational programmers are not only unhinged from the place of their origin but also oriented more generally to a place different from their immediate physical and cultural location. This subjectivity thrives on "difference," as expressed in the longing for the "other" national space. One looks out, as if from a bird cage, to the sky of one's desired flight. The cage in question is that of national closure, whose institutional doors open and shut to let the immigrant subject in or out. The cage thus is also a cage of identity closure, which the transnational subject at once embraces and desires to escape. One embraces national identity as a refuge from the ever-shifting grounds of a mobile world, as reflected in the following statement of a programmer who at the time was working in the United States: "The smell of Indian soil is not found anywhere in the world." Yet one also wishes to escape from its consequences by keeping one's permanent residency in the United States intact. The subjectivity discussed here is not the kind that when given a chance allows persons to recognize their natural home. It is a troubled existential space, which is at least in some measure the result of practices of flexible labor that are inherently wedded to temporary settlements and fleeting commitments. As bodies are shipped across continents by the new transnational order of capital, the new order also helps to generate in the process different souls that are forever nostalgic for the other home.

Systemic Flexibility and Body Shopping

Although the transnational immigrant condition has its upbeat moments, it constantly negotiates systemic demands of flexibility and the unsettling social effects that result. Caught between twin systems of transnational capitalism pressing for a free flow of labor and the system of the state that has nationalistic concerns, immigrant lives must forgo plans for stability and permanence. The H-1B visa issued to programmers so that they can enter and work in the United States cannot be extended beyond six years. Although visa holders can apply for permanent residency while working for a company, it takes a couple of years for their application to be decided, without any guarantee of approval. It is also difficult to settle down and start a family during this period. As one of the software professionals explained, "While going on an H1 visa to the U.S., your wife cannot work. She is restricted to the home and that has also been one of the . . . pressures." The regime also discourages immigrants from having children, because of their uncertain future as well as the possibility that their children will need to contend with different systems of education in India and the United States. As a result, most programmers tend to be young and single. In addition, the bureaucratic apparatus of the nation-state puts further demands on transnational lives in general, including people with immigrant and nonimmigrant visas as well as applicants for permanent residency. For even a minor inquiry, some may have to stand in line as early as four or five o'clock in the morning at the Bureau of Citizenship and Immigration Services (BCIS, formerly the Immigration and Naturalization Service), sometimes braving the rain or snow for five or six hours; others must get fingerprinted for various purposes on short notice.

At times, ignorance of a minor provision of law may lead to major humiliation. On 20 January 2000 INS agents arrested forty Indian programmers—including ten women, two of them pregnant—in a raid at a U.S. Air Force base. INS officials said that the raid came after a six-month probe into visa violations, which involved promises to the government by companies to place highly skilled foreign workers in jobs that did not yet exist; the workers were then sent to other workplaces. The programmers belonged to a team of 320 engineers who were building new software for Air Force personnel data systems in San Antonio. One of the engineers arrested, Chandrasekhar Reddy, recalled: "[The INS agents] handcuffed each one of us, including the pregnant women, although we did not offer any resistance. . . . It was a very humiliating experience. We were paraded like common criminals. An official refused to open my handcuffs so that I could use the rest room. His answer was, 'You may stab me with a pen and flee'" (Easwaran 2000). Allegedly, some of the arrests were the result of noncompliance with the technical legality of a Labor Condition Application (LCA), which requires that employers place their workers only at a location for which the LCA was approved. Under scrutiny, the incident illustrates an ever-present but growing tension between governance schemes that inform transnational capital and those that animate the nation-state. In a competitively structured field of capitalism, body shopping and just-in-time labor are important schemes to tap globally dispersed cheap labor while avoiding the overhead costs of large labor inventory. However, the existing institutional setup of the modern nation-state, despite a long partnership with transnational capitalism, still relies on a categorical closure between the citizen and the alien. To protect the citizen, it must restrict the alien's field of operation and mobility.

Migration thus emerges as a site of conflict between various forces. Certain state agencies are pressured to facilitate labor immigration while others are forced to police and restrict it. There are two interrelated pressures to recruit foreign labor. First, transnational capitalism demands the quicker and easier flow of labor across national spaces; second, as the economic performance in advanced capitalistic democracies has become the ground for their legitimation, the state is hard-pressed to reduce wage pressure and thus inflation during economic upswings by recruiting foreign labor. However, there are also pressures—both nationalistic and democratic—on other state institutions to ensure job security and stability in the lifeworld of citizens by restricting and policing the world of immigrants. In this field of conflicting interests, forces of resistance against exploitation are also pitted against each other. While labor unions oppose cheap foreign labor and thus favor limits on immigration as an act of resistance against capitalistic efforts to reduce and replace local workers, immigration activist groups resist the systematic exploitation of foreign workers resulting from such limits.

Broadly, the field of body shopping is facilitated by systemic forces of transnational capitalism, including corporate lobbying, employment, advertising, and media-induced incitement as well as the activities of state agencies like U.S. Citizenship and Immigration Services (formerly the INS) and the visa-granting division of the Department of State. The programming of migration also includes policing by the Bureau of Citizenship and Immigration Services and other state agencies such as the Employment and Training Administration and the Employment Standards Administration (both in the Department of Labor) with a view to achieving controlled results. However, the systemically induced and carefully orchestrated migration is not harmonious. It is contested by forces claiming to protect citizens (e.g., labor unions and anti-immigration groups) and immigrants (immigrant advocacy groups). The complex field of migration complicates traditional alignments of allies and adversaries. For example, the language of the AFL-CIO starts resembling that of relatively conservative groups like the Federation of American Immigration Reform (FAIR). Despite recent pro-immigrant moments, the AFL-CIO has advocated "halting the expansion of the guest-worker [H-1B] program, which allows companies to recruit foreign workers when there is a shortage of workers with a particular skill. Too often, these programs are used to discriminate against American workers, depress wages and distort labor markets. A better solution would be to train American workers for the jobs that exist" (AFL-CIO 2001).

Similarly, FAIR, a conservative, nationalist group, proposed a "moratorium" on immigration and claimed that "the 'labor shortage' was created by the IT Industry itself in its attempts to maximize profits . . . Our government's policy should be directed to wean the industry off its quick fix and ac-

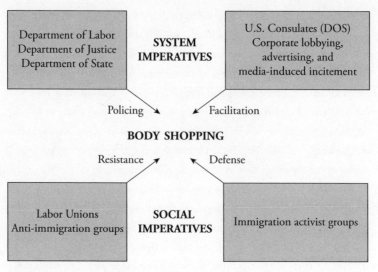

FIGURE 2. *Body shopping as a site of contest.*

custom it to cultivating a homegrown workforce" (Federation for American Immigration Reform 2000). Many other conservative and nationalist groups like American Patrol and the California Coalition for Immigration Reform have been involved in anti-immigration activism. As Saskia Sassen points out: "Economic globalization denationalizes national economies; in contrast, immigration is re-nationalizing politics" (Sassen 1996, 59). Both liberal (AFL-CIO) and conservative (FAIR) resistance to immigration may be characterized as a response to the destabilization of citizens' social worlds by a system that demands more flexibility from both immigrant and citizen. Despite their common nationalist cloak, the two responses are underpinned by different rationales: worker protection and the dangerous politics of identity. Let us look at body shopping as a site of contest among different forces.

Figure 2 illustrates how transnational corporations and certain state institutions facilitate as well as police the flow of immigrants to achieve greater systemic integration. While labor unions and nationalist groups resist immigration in general, immigration activist and human rights groups guard against rigid policing that could hurt immigrants who already lack the rights enjoyed by citizens. The efforts of labor unions have resulted in many conditions imposed by the Department of Labor on the employment of H-1B workers. First, employers are prohibited from replacing U.S. citizens with H-1B workers, and from placing H-1B workers at other employers' work sites where U.S. citizens have been displaced. Second, employers must make good faith efforts to hire qualified U.S. citizens before hiring H-1B workers and to hire citizens if they are at least as qualified as the H-1B workers whom they intend to employ (this provision is governed by the Department of Justice). Third, employers must attest that they are not involved in a strike, lockout, or work stoppage in the course of a labor dispute, as the Department of Labor wants to ensure that H-1B workers are not hired as a tactic to replace workers on strike. In fact, employers must not place, assign, lease, or otherwise contract out an H-1B worker, during the LCA's validity, to any place of employment where there is a strike or lockout in the course of a labor dispute involving the same occupations as those to which the LCA applies. In administering these restrictions the state seems to lack its fabled unity, as the agencies that aim to facilitate immigration are apt to criticize other agencies, such as the Department of Labor, for transcending their bounds by unilaterally imposing new rules as they seek to police immigrant labor.

This micro-governance of embodied immigration, despite the flexibility of immigration and employment policies, does hinder the flexibility inherent in body shopping. Thus, surprising as it may seem, body shopping is not flexible enough for an emerging transnational labor regime. Body shopping still involves actual border crossing as well as authorization and policing by agencies of the nation-state. In the context of programming labor, a new regime of virtual labor migration is slowly emerging as an alternative, more flexible means of securing a flow of labor from India to the United States. Under this system, labor bypasses the state borders while the immigrant's body stays within national territorial spaces. In fact the decline in body shopping is directly linked to the rise of offshore virtual engagements, bringing these practices together as two alternate forms of labor supply. Many informants noted a gradual shift from body shopping to offshore project development, especially with the rise of reliable and fast communication links. The annual review of Nasscom (the National Association of Software and Service Companies) directly connects the practice of body shopping (on-site development) with virtual labor flows (offshore development), pointing out how the offshore component of work is increasing because of "unnatural visa restrictions enforced by the U. S." as well as the availability of high-speed data communication links: "In 1988, the percentage of onsite development [through body shopping] was almost as high as 90 percent. During 1999–2000, the offshore component is expected to increase to about 45 percent of total software exports" (Nasscom 2000, 22). In 2004 the virtual flow of labor finally surpassed the on-site performance of work. The next chapter analyzes how virtual migration provides a fresh horizon for viewing the changing forms of system integration through a different arrangement of space and time.

CHAPTER 4

Virtual Migration

All that is solid melts into air . . . —Marx and Engels (1848)

Electronic aids, particularly domestic computers, will help the inner migration, the opting out of reality. Reality is no longer going to be the stuff *out there*, but the stuff inside your head. It's going to be commercial and nasty at the same time. —J. G. Ballard (1971)

Not all that is solid has melted into air, and poor reality, though besieged and beleaguered, still seems to matter. Wars are still written in blood. Self-assured skyscrapers and streets crowded with ostentatious cars are all quite solid and real. Perhaps the question is not about the solidity of reality but rather about its dependence on programming schemes, which precede and govern it. From simulated models of cars to models of economy, the production of solid reality increasingly traces its roots to the virtual. There is a rising tendency to see the world through virtual schemes and then act in ways that make the real conform to the virtual (Carrier and Miller 1998). Economic models do not simply describe an existing, empirical state of affairs; rather, they are performative. For instance, in the world of finance the Black-Scholes-Merton option pricing equation altered traders' behavior and pricing patterns in a way that made itself more true over time (MacKenzie 2003). The equation did not merely represent but performed the real. A simpler example would be the theoretical assumption of economic models that humans are rational, competitive, and calculating individuals. A competitive system based on this model produces such individuals by making difficult the survival of noncompetitive and noncalculative behavior within the system.

While the real may be increasingly virtual in conception, the virtual sounds more and more real and physical. Cyberspace is full of physical, geographical, and even organic metaphors: site, space, property, window, Navigator, Explorer, superhighway, shopping carts, traffic, spiders, viruses, and worms—the list is long. Lest you think these are mere metaphors, there have been lawsuits in the United States construing cyberspace as physical space: for example, eBay charged Bidder's Edge with "trespass" in a lawsuit for collecting information from its "site" with the help of spiders or bots (programs that run on remote machines), which entered eBay's website despite the signs prohibiting "entry." As absurd as it may sound, eBay's lawyer argued that trespass law is especially suitable to virtual space, because it is easy to establish clear signs about which activities are prohibited and because the site is owned by eBay not merely in its virtual form but also in a physical form (as machines or servers).

Virtual migration is equally complicated. When labor moves from machine to machine across nations, it is hard to capture in conventional categories (as in the case above), since conventional labor migration is generally situated within the framework of body migration. The continuous revolutionizing of the instruments of production, distribution, and consumption has enabled a new labor regime in which labor moves and migrates without the worker's body. The physical ways of performing work are not going to vanish: just as the theater did not disappear after the cinema turned acting bodies into moving pictures, the embodied migration of labor will perhaps never be replaced by virtual labor flows, as some services can be performed only with the body. Virtual and physical migrations are drastically different species in their mode of global integration, even if they tend to produce similar economic effects in terms of jobs and wages. They are as different as cyberspace is from physical space, despite court cases and metaphors to the contrary.

The rules of the road for virtual migration differ from those for physical migration such as body shopping. When a programmer in Delhi accesses a client's machine in New Jersey, we may define her presence in the United States as virtual presence or tele-presence, but clearly not as physical presence. In fact, computer networks—pathways of virtual migration—are so insensitive to geography that it is almost impossible to determine the exact physical location of the machine without extraneous knowledge. The network is technologically indifferent to physical location. Knowing the location of the client's machine may even be irrelevant to the programmer's task.

Network Interface Cards may have "physical addresses" and computers may be assigned IP addresses, but these are logical addresses that identify the machine on the network, not in real space. True, the network's design may be changed to add a provision for filtering and screening for specific geographic tags in packet headers. One could, for example, instruct the machine to refuse access to requests originating from the domain ".in" (India). But one should not think of the ".in" home page as a physical home, because a person may be sitting anywhere while managing the ".in" website. The body is never in cyberspace in any practical sense, and constraints are not physical but only logical and programmable. Indeed, companies tend to distribute their resources on many machines around the world that can be seamlessly accessed by the worker without knowledge of their exact physical location. There is no consistent homology between cyberspace and physical space (Mitchell 1996), except that both may be designed, integrated, and controlled through programming schemes (e.g., street planning schemes for physical space or software scripts for cyberspace). Cyberspace, even in its drastic difference, does connect and integrate physical worlds far apart, linking labor from one world to another.

There are two specific aspects of the virtual migration of software labor: spatial integration, which decouples work performance and the work site, and temporal integration, a real-time unification of different time zones, which underscores the importance of the temporal point of the revolving and rotating earth where one is located.

Spatial Integration

The programming schemes of virtual integration do not entail transporting the body from one place to another; instead, they keep the body in one place while performance travels to other locations. Virtual labor migration is not a single scheme of integration. It may range from the real-time work performed on mainframe computers and servers in the United States by a worker based in India to a distributed work design, allowing a firm to be geographically dispersed, without a central work station, among several sites throughout the world. Such a firm may divide up its work to take advantage of cheaper labor, diverse skills, and different time zones. Different modules of the system can be independently developed and electronically combined.

This programming labor is both an effect and cause of global integrations. On the one hand, virtual programming labor owes its origin to the transnational capitalist drive to harness cheaper skilled labor outside national borders by novel means; on the other hand, this form of labor—with universal and systems-level programming schemes—further integrates pockets of the world by tightening the interconnectedness of labor, capital, and administration in functional supply chains. One of the project managers in New Delhi described how the managers helped the Gap to develop a new information system to track its orders and connect its globally scattered vendors: "What Gap does is, like, all their clothes are produced in the Third World, Latin America, India, Bangladesh and all these countries. They have vendors in all these places, so purchase orders are created between these vendors and Gap, and you want to purchase so many goods of a certain style, cut, size, and this order is sent out to these vendors. So, the process of automation is purchase order creation, and then getting the goods back and things like that. We were involved in the development activity. Gap had given us a complete project. We cloned their environment on our own mainframe. We . . . developed the complete software, and then I was in the U.S. implementing it and making changes." Offshore programming labor thus is not merely a consequence of system imperatives. By creating software-based programming schemes that integrate various units around the world, it is a major force behind transnational system integration. It is responsible for creating integrative spaces that ground a variety of work flows and transactions related to banking, insurance, financial services, manufacturing, retail, distribution, communications, government, transport, and hotels.

With enough bandwidth, labor in India has been integrated into American corporate sites twenty thousand miles away, reducing an enormous spatial gulf to a matter of faster or slower transmission speeds. In 2004 there were more than eight hundred firms in India providing virtual labor to corporations in the United States and other countries. Nearly a decade ago the *Economist* (1996) reported that more than a hundred of America's top five hundred firms bought software services from firms in India. In 2001–02 about half a million workers were employed by the Indian IT industry, which is mostly oriented to foreign markets and has the majority of its clients in the United States. Over 200,000 workers were employed in global software development, while 106,000 others provided a staggering array of related services, including customer service, banking, financial and credit analysis, back-office accounting and other operations, data entry, data conversion, transcription, translation, technical support, animation, engineering and design, website development and maintenance, remote education, electronic marketing, data search and integration, market research, documentation handling, and human resource services like employee benefits and payroll. The National Association of Software and Service Companies, or Nasscom, claims to be a "truly global trade body with around 850 members, of which nearly 150 are global companies from the US, UK, EU, Japan and China" operating from India. Most of these companies are global because the domestic market for software and services is very small compared to the offshore market, which offers major work contracts for Indian-based firms. Close to 60 percent of the revenues of the software and services market flows from foreign sources, jumping from $9.55 billion in 2002–3 to an estimated $12.2 billion in 2003–4 (Nasscom 2004).

We may understand the scheme of on-site labor that physically migrates from India through body shopping or otherwise as one mode of labor supply, and online labor that migrates from India virtually as another. Contrary to common categorization, I do not place the two in separate realms of migration and trade. In fact, both forms of labor are combined at times in carrying out a single project. A firm in India might send two or three systems analysts to the client's site in the United States for a short period, so that they might gain a first-hand understanding of the project and discuss systems design. These systems analysts then help to develop the project in India while remaining constantly in touch with their client, who can monitor the progress of the project and provide input. Once the project is over, one or two programmers fly back to the United States to test the system and oversee its installation.

A variety of transnational business strategies have evolved to integrate and govern dispersed labor. In many cases American companies have either entered into joint ventures with Indian companies or subcontracted part of their work to Indian companies while maintaining continuous electronic contact. A large number of Indian software professionals are connected to the mainframe computers of their American clients from a remote location, completing a series of back-end jobs every day when the system in the United States is not as busy.[1] Some large insurance companies in the United States that receive a huge number of claims get their processing done through such a virtual mode of spatial integration. This ability to perform work at a place other than the location of the laboring body is becoming more and more common, not only in the context of third-party outsourcing but also among companies based in two or more locations.

When problems or glitches occur, however, the model does not always work smoothly. Many companies combine online labor with onsite support. One systems analyst cited an instance when his team supported Citibank operations: "Citibank had [changed] all their retail business; there were a lot of changes required in the programs already existing like day-to-day maintenance . . . One way is that they have their own people do it. The other way is how the work in their bank in Japan was done . . . There was a team of people working in India, and there was a project manager on site [in Japan]. I was the project manager, I would take work from the Japanese managers and I would send it offshore to India . . . So any changes, any production problems, anything will immediately come to [notice through] me."

To avoid problems of coordination, Indian firms developed what was known as a 75–25 model. While 75 percent of their work force remained in India, they established a small office in the United States, comprising the remaining 25 percent of the work force, to coordinate and mediate between the Indian team and the American client. One major software company in Bombay, which also had a small unit in the United States, provided twenty-four-hour information systems management for insurance claims processing to a major American insurance company by accessing its mainframe computer directly from India. One programmer, who moved briefly from Bombay to North Carolina while working for the same company, described this software work as follows: "The Bombay team can directly access the client's mainframe. Usually what we have is maintenance project, and we support [the firm's] insurance business for twenty-four hours . . . There are different groups in [the firm], and [we] support most of them . . . So, suppose someone is claiming [insurance] money from [the insurance company] due to some accident. He would go to [the firm's] agents, [who] would enter the data on [Customer Information Control System] screens, [inputs] like where this accident happened, what's the cause, and other details of the accident. And when this information is entered on CICS screens and the daytime is over in the USA, that information is captured and is written to a file, which is the input for our nightly batch processing."

In terms of work performed, there is no critical difference between onshore labor engagements (North Carolina) and offshore ones (Mumbai), even if the first is characterized as migration and the second as trade. Software firms see on-site and online methods of labor supply as interchangeable "components" of the same transnational programming labor. Granted, the classification of onshore labor as "migration" and offshore labor as "trade" serves a function in the existing institutional setup of nation states; virtual labor remains a systemic innovation to negotiate national borders in a different way, using the same pool of Indian programmers.

In addition to constant support, maintenance, and enhancement of information systems, Indian software companies also work on independent software projects by cloning the client's systems environment—a unique feature of information technologies—and then redesigning and reengineering the system. The client could be a bank, an airline, or a manufacturer.

[margin handwritten note: Conclusion]

Another strategy of integration uses a third firm to connect through its common software platform a firm based in the United States to a firm based in India: "[This firm] helps companies source and deploy virtual skills to deliver work on time and on budget. Through [the firm's] technology, customers gain access to an outsourced workforce that is globally competitive, cost-effective, high-quality, fluid and flexible. Through [the firm's] proprietary technology platform, the geographic constraint is removed from the traditional, bricks-and-mortar staffing paradigm, allowing companies, for the first time, to deploy a virtual staff."

In some cases, American companies set up subsidiaries in India for various purposes, ranging from high-end research collaboration with American-based teams (a common pattern with Adobe and Microsoft) to low-end programming work to converting already documented tasks into software, as well as providing technical, financial, and customer services on line and on the phone (as is often done by the American International Group and GE Capital). Instead of using the binary terminology of "high-end" and "low-end" programming, I have elsewhere described the whole range of programming skills along a spectrum from less saturated skills to more saturated skills (Aneesh 2001). I have proposed that the problem of skill should be analyzed in terms not of high or low skills but of the closure of play space in the structure of skills, which I term "skill saturation." This is a phenomenon characterized by an absolute predictability of procedure and outcome, resulting from an exhaustive ordering of various components of skills, and the elimination of all irregular spaces of work. On a spectrum from higher saturation to lower saturation, one could identify two kinds of programming: programming for a definite task, and programming for an imagined outcome. The first implies relatively saturated skills, as it consists chiefly of translating and codifying an already known task (such as an accounting or banking procedure) into a software package, where all the elements of the system are known and the creativity consists only in creating a simple and efficient program. Writing software for an imagined outcome—for example, designing a chip with an imagined higher processing power—is, on the other hand, a task for which no procedure has yet been identified, implying a relatively unsaturated skill. Software companies in India are engaged in both kinds of work. At the less saturated end, one CEO of an Indian subsidiary of an American company claimed that the kind of work done in India might be more advanced, dealing with more abstract, newer, imagined problems: "Well, we are part of [the firm's] engineering team. The work that gets done here is the same as is being . . . in the U.S. with a little bit of difference. The difference might be that the work we do here is slightly better quality than what gets done in the U.S., . . . [where] there is a bunch of work that's maintenance, it's maintaining old components and old tools. We would not take up too much of old things; we would start from scratch, newer things . . . So in that sense the kind of projects that we are getting here are slightly better quality than what people probably have on an average in the U.S."

The less saturated software engineering forms a smaller proportion of programming work carried out in India, as the majority of Indian companies are engaged in work involving more saturated skills. At the more saturated and routine end of the programming spectrum, one software professional in Noida, India, mentioned writing and customizing software for already existing tasks, like banking procedures: "We support your daily requirements for banking applications like daily branch opening, your account handling, your money transfers, everything, the routine tasks for which there's a need to build the software. It's very routine because most rules are documented. You just have to implement those business rules into software programs."

Toward the unsaturated end of the programming spectrum were some high-tech American and European firms (Adobe, Microsoft, Lucent, Siemens, and Nokia) that connected their spatially dispersed teams through data communication links, integrating their parts as if they were adjacent rooms in the same building where two teams might be working on the same project. "There are twenty people working in the U.S. and twenty people in India," said one CEO, describing the mechanisms of online collaboration between his team in India and its counterpart in the United States. "They are doing different things. But the mother ship is the same; it goes into the same product. So you are working on the same database, you are working on the same code. You are working on the same thing . . . we are sharing . . . a data server [and] we are working on those systems. Except for the fact that we are in India, we could be sitting across the room from those people and working."

The phrase "sitting across the room" was not a passive statement about global connectivity; rather, it was a continuing activity that joined the discourse of integration with the continuous production and refinement of corresponding equipment and apparatus. All major companies persistently invested in installing and upgrading data communication lines that allowed for virtual work flows. The emerging labor regime depends heavily on this mode of integration, which affords a new architecture for transnational strategies of organizational governance. More and more companies are investing in direct and dedicated communication links, as reflected in the following statement of the vice-president of another software firm in Noida, India: "Since we have a dedicated satellite, and we have paid for our lines, we are not dependent on any indirect channels; we have direct channels, if you want to speak to the U.S. I can put you through within half a minute; I don't even have to dial the [area] codes . . . so that's the kind of dedicated link I'm talking about. It's called the link line; that's how our server, our computers are connected." Globalization, in view of these concrete practices, does not come across as a passive force of history or an inevitable phenomenon happening behind our backs. Rather it is enacted, implemented, and brought about through such integration schemes, resulting from the actions of high-level executives who consciously deploy technologies of integration. These technologies are constantly refined and upgraded.

Programming labor in India combines with other kinds of labor to provide services such as legal database support to large American law firms. Many Indian software firms armed with locally trained lawyers work closely, though remotely, with law firms in the United States to develop software-based databases of easily accessible legal information, equipped with common criteria to incorporate new documents. Similarly, in development of digital content such as animation, the content provider, while based in the United States, is able to continually review the project being developed in India. Other projects that employ the continuous integration of spatially separate units involve the development of web content, computer aided design and manufacturing (CAD-CAM), and saturated skills like medical transcriptions for American doctors who electronically send dictation through high-speed data communication lines. Since the late 1990s IT-enabled services in general, and call centers in particular, have added enormously to virtual labor flows across the national borders of India and the United States. Included in such virtual flows are customer service interactions through call centers, business process management, back-office operations, insurance claims processing, medical transcriptions, legal databases, payroll, human resource services, web site services, data digitization, online education, and digital content.

Although IT-enabled services consist of mostly saturated skills, they provide a vivid example of virtual migration. Using dedicated, leased telecommunication lines, workers at remote call centers in India connect to the parent organization through voice links and online database access. This form of transnational, virtual labor flows is as direct as telecommuting within the boundaries of the national state. For example, when a bank customer in the United States calls the bank's customer service number, the call is immediately redirected to Indian locations without the customer's knowledge. The respondent in India taps into the customer's history and customer-owned product attributes, using the latest technological developments in global online information systems and web-enabled databases. Call centers in India handle complaints, technical queries, customer relations, account management, sales leads and follow-ups, telemarketing, credit and billing problems, market research, and database development. These services are used by airlines, hospitals, law firms, utilities, and companies engaged in finance telecommunications, insurance, high technology, and manufacturing. Some companies set up their own subsidiaries to harness Indian labor. GE Capital has a subsidiary in Gurgaon, near New Delhi, that manages payroll accounting, call centers, mortgage-based loans, and insurance claims for consumers in the United States.

Lest I gave the impression that this kind of labor integration takes place only between two countries such as India and the United States, I should point out another transnational strategy that distributes software development to many sites around the world. Each site might work on a different stage of a product's life cycle; or the sites might divide responsibility along developmental lines, with one working on the application engineering, including specifications analysis, design, and integration and acceptance testing, and another site implementing system components; or the work might be distributed according to the qualifications of the team at each site. One Indian team employed by a subsidiary of an American firm worked on a project with five teams based in such faraway places as Tokyo, Singapore, Sydney, Beijing, and Arlington Heights. The global networking of labor has increasingly become the norm rather than the exception in software development.

Managed by the programming schemes of Internet protocols and applications, networks increasingly dominate socioeconomic life. "For the first time in history," Manuel Castells asserts, "the basic unit of economic organization is not a subject, be it individual (such as the entrepreneur, or entrepreneurial family) or collective (such as the capitalistic class, the corporation, the state) . . . the unit is the network, made up of a variety of subjects and organizations, relentlessly modified as networks adapt to supportive environments and market structures" (Castells 1996, 214).

The global mobility of labor increasingly depends on networks of this sort. As corporations evermore exist in direct networks with their suppliers and customers, it is less meaningful to talk about economic organization in terms of separate units rather than networked labor, information, and capital. The networking strategies have imparted enormous flexibility to the system, but to reap the full benefits of network flexibility, "the corporation," Castells (1996, 176) points out, "had to become a network itself and dynamize each element of its internal structure." Interorganizational computer networks have attracted particular attention among organizational analysts (Benjamin, Delong, and Morton 1990; Benjamin, Rociiart, Morton, and Wyman 1984; Keen 1986; Meyer and Boone 1987; Zaheer and Venkatraman 1994), who have focused especially on electronic data interchange (EDI) in business-related transactions. However, as I have tried to show, EDI now covers real-time work flows, including exchanges related to design and manufacturing activities (Hart and Estrin 1991). Castells's attempt to understand the emerging economic regime in terms of networks has two advantages: first, it avoids the national-global dichotomy that has clouded most debates on globalization, as I pointed out in chapter 2. Second, the idea of networks enables an analysis based on flows, rather than isolated units, entities, and individuals, thereby bringing out the intrinsic interdependence of different economic processes and their relationship with the social world.

However, discussions of organizational networks tend to be economistic, focusing on possible efficiencies, competitive advantage, coordination, and relative transaction costs for corporations (Benjamin, Delong, and Morton 1990; Benjamin, Rockart, Morton, and Wyman 1984; Hart and Estrin 1991; Meyer and Boone 1987; Zaheer and Venkatraman 1994). The same is true of such conventional concepts as outsourcing and subcontracting. Inserting the practice of virtual labor migration into traditional schemata and concepts—such as outsourcing and subcontracting—makes it difficult to develop an understanding independent of corporate needs and motives. Surely, a business may need to "outsource" and "subcontract" work to reduce the size of its permanent work force or capitalize on globally dispersed low-cost labor. But any analysis based on functional choices made by corporations within the competitively structured field of capitalism tends to hide the politics of technologies. Public and corporate choices for particular technologies are also choices for particular social orders (Winner 1986), in this case a global social order with social effects going beyond corporate interests. A concrete description of the practice may reveal social consequences and adjustments that are not easily visible in analyses based solely on the perspectives of business needs and processes.

The language of "networks," despite its many advantages, also seems a little too neutral and objective, much as it does in the computer sciences, obscuring relations of power and governance in the emerging regime. To discern the social consequences of growing system integration through networks, we need to closely look at adjustments made essential in social life by the velocity of electronic transmissions, which transform the space-time dimensions of social and work life. Recent breakthroughs in the transnational organization of labor are due to advances in the velocity of work flows, as well as to such developments as the programming of different organizational possibilities. These developments are not without their internal problems. Horizontal global integrations are beset with snags. They fail to work as often as they succeed.

Horizontal Disconnect

I asked the vice-president of a software company in New Delhi why on-site services had not completely given way to online services. "Because the management [in U.S. corporations] is many times lazy in providing complete systems specifications," he replied, a statement that is only partly true. Of course firms must precisely formulate requirements for transnationally developed software and agree upon modest quality standards, usually by entering into a contract; they must develop detailed specifications and project definitions, including methods, schedule, scope, and deliverables, clearly understood and agreed to by both parties. But there are many other reasons why the physical flow of migrants continues despite virtual labor integration. The instantaneous flow of labor from India to the United States simultaneously facilitates and hampers work organization along space and time dimensions. By decoupling work performance from the site of work, virtual integration overcomes distances, but only by losing the rich, multilayered, face-to-face interaction provided by place-based integration at work. Companies attempt to recover this loss of spatio-temporal immediacy by various mechanisms such as direct phone connections, video conferencing, electronic message boards, and instant messaging, as well as limited on-site visits. Indian software professionals are often flown to the United States for a brief initial meeting with the client, as it is not always possible for the client to formulate complete project specifications and communicate them online. Similarly, at the end of the project, despite the online access to completed software projects, senior software engineers typically return to the United States to ensure the successful implementation of their projects. Even short business trips for emergency meetings can create problems related to visas, work restrictions, or different systems of social security. Schemes of integration based on the nation-state model come into conflict with global integrations. Physical migration thus must be planned in advance.

Physical migration is also required if knowledge of the project requires understanding other components of the system and the enterprise. "[When] you are developing a project, which interfaces to a lot of other projects within the U.S.," an informant noted, "those interfaces have to be studied there only . . . You can't just ship it here. If you ship it here . . . it's very difficult for the people to understand what the interfaces are; there [could be] ten different departments interfacing with this department." Often face-to-face communication is very important for a quick resolution of problems. Even when problems are resolvable by e-mail or phone, software companies in India depend on senior project managers who have been to the United States and understand American styles and speech. Virtual integration cannot instantly overcome sociocultural differences. Another software professional admitted that it was difficult for programmers sitting in India to understand what the client wanted, because of their limited knowledge of the United States in general. One responsibility of the senior project manager is often to translate phone and e-mail communications: "[In the U.S.] people can resolve things through meetings, through discussions, through lectures, through face-to-face interaction," a project manager explained. "[Here in India] communication does become a problem . . . the entry-level people are the people who haven't been to the U.S. or who haven't been abroad; they can't really relate . . . So you always require a senior person, a project manager who can relate to what the Americans mean."

It is not surprising, as mentioned earlier, that many Indian software companies also set up smaller offices in the United States for effective coordination and communication between their developers in India and the clients in the United States. "There is something to be said about face-to-face communication," another programmer emphasized, "being in face-to-face communication, and being part of the team physically is very different from being just online." Face-to-face encounters, especially informal corridor talk at work, are surely of a different order. Karin Knorr Cetina and Urs Bruegger

(2002) have introduced an appropriate distinction between embodied presence and response presence. Embodied presence is always face to face; but response presence describes situations in which the participants are capable of responding to one another and common objects in real time without being physically present in the same place. Being interactionally present through the screen does not mean that one can discuss things over a cup of coffee with colleagues across the globe or share a hearty laugh with the team on the other side of the video screen; audiovisual links fail to carry jokes over to the other side. At current technological levels, the screen does tend to split the teams, making it improbable for a single social space—or at least the usual social space—to emerge. In the absence of what Alfred Schutz (1973) described as the "interlocking of the glances" and the "thousand-faceted mirroring of each other," many sociocultural differences, including different first languages among developers in remote locations, are exacerbated in audiovisual gatherings. But we must also not forget that the screen allows a kind of gathering not possible in face-to-face situations. Before the advent of software platforms, it was not possible for so many workers, managers, and developers to watch the same screen and make changes to the same database. In the realm of financial integration, Karin Knorr Cetina and Urs Bruegger (2002) rightly assert that only the screen's emergence made it possible for traders to simultaneously watch the market.

Virtual migration presents a problem of synchrony across sociocultural and physical divides. In the heat of continued success, one must not forget that the Indian software industry also hides many failed projects and abandoned transnational business relationships. Heeks, Krishna, Nicholson, and Sahay (2001) define quite accurately the question of success or failure in global software relationships as "synching or sinking," defining how congruence must be achieved along six dimensions (the initials of which form the mnemonic "cockpit"): coordination and control systems, objectives and values, capabilities, processes, information, and technology. Organizational relationships across the globe must synchronize themselves along these dimensions or they will sink. Clearly, the synchronization must be programmed by structuring work with clear specifications; it must also be performed by making attitudes, values, and organizational behavior work in unison. To develop successful software systems together, the client in the United

States must transfer some of its knowledge and technology to the subcontractor in India, as well as synchronize its management systems and organizational culture. Studying the relationship between the American company Global and its Indian counterpart Shiva, Heeks, Krishna, Nicholson, and Sahay (2001, 56) found that Shiva had a relatively personalized and subjective management culture while Global's stressed objectivity and accountability. "It took enormous efforts before the Shiva project leader would produce a standardized monthly progress report, and Shiva staff refused to participate in Global's employee satisfaction survey." Evidently sociocultural differences could not be easily erased.

When problems occurred because of sociocultural differences, the solutions increasingly took a technical turn. The introduction of such external quality standards as the Capability Maturity Model (CMM), developed by the Software Engineering Institute at Carnegie-Mellon University, and the ISO 9000 series, developed by the International Organization for Standardization, served the purpose of "objectivity" over the years. These standards were used by software firms in India as a label for their quality and performance. There were also other ways to program some sociocultural differences out of the system, though not all. While it may be difficult to extract a programmer's performance report from an Indian project manager, it is increasingly possible to program some functions of monitoring into the system itself. For example, software development platforms have acquired a defect-tracking function that can identify the number of errors made per thousand lines of code.

Despite the development of external standards and the coding of governance structures into software platforms, there have been numerous barriers, both social and physical in nature, that have hindered systemic integration. A temporal lag in data communication links does not help the cause of synchrony. One CEO complained of the slow and overpriced connections provided by the Indian state as he discussed his plans to install, as far as the law permitted, his own fiberoptic lines, which were vital for the virtual integration of remote sites: "Our work—because we are completely integrated—requires something like 100 Mbps or 200 Mbps; what we get is 256K at an exorbitant price. And because it's going through a satellite, there is a delay. There is a ping time of 300 or 400 milliseconds,[2] which is too high for our kind of work. So, what we want is go all the way on fiberoptics, so that we can ping at 7 or 8 milliseconds. That'll improve the response of a lot of our systems." The system has reached a stage where a delay of 300–400 milliseconds, hardly noticeable to previous generations, has become crucial in the programming of globalization. Quite like technologies of material mobility, virtual migration must contend with the question of time and speed as the forever receding frontier of spatial conquest.

The question of speed is not new. "[The] history of capitalism has been characterized by a speed-up in the pace of life, while so overcoming spatial barriers that the world sometimes seems to collapse inwards upon us" (Harvey 1989, 240). David Harvey (1989) employs the concept of "time-space compression" to describe how faster modes of transport have drastically reduced the size of the world by annihilating space through time. The experience of time-space compression is not merely a physical experience in the form, for instance, of jet lag; it also translates into accelerating turnover time in production and a parallel quickening in exchange and consumption, with the associated rise of temporariness in all spheres of life. At the speed of light, the electromagnetic waves of virtual mobility take the time-space compression to another level. As distances become transparent, a new form of space compression reduces the need for movement from one place to the other, and time compression makes more work available at any one point of time. This integration is different from the material integration of space attained through air transport, for example. The difference is not only that between the flow of physical bodies and bodies of code; it is also one of speed. Being a logical entity, code rides on electromagnetic waves close to the velocity of light, connecting spaces in "real time." High as it may seem, the speed at which data flows is impeded by many factors (such as data traffic and the low quality of cables), resulting in brief but annoying delays that seem foregrounded in functional schemes of integration; by the time delays are reduced for one type of dataflow (such as text), other forms of data (such as images or video) start competing for the increased bandwidth. We must remember that virtual migration does not merely suffer from the problem of delay; it constitutes the very possibility of delay. In the absence of virtual integration, complaints about slow connections in India would obviously not be raised.

The drive to increase the speed and bandwidth of online transmissions leads to a related dimension: time. This is another underexamined subject in labor and globalization studies: the programmed integration of workers' lived time. The distinction between spatial and temporal integration is mostly analytical, as they are two aspects of the same phenomenon. In step with the relativity of space-time dimensions, the sheer velocity of dataflow integrates spatially dispersed places while also bringing days and nights of different temporal horizons within a single framework. A global regime of "real time" increasingly presides over the previously secluded temporal pockets of life. Discourses of the "local" become possible only against an overarching global canopy.

Temporal Integration: Follow the Sun

The speed of electronic flows brings different time zones together and connects them in real time. Work is integrated across geographies, aided by the logic of programming schemes, including information protocols that facilitate electronic flows through adaptive routing. These protocols periodically reevaluate the fastest route between two points in the network, taking stock of the current traffic in the network, broken routes, and other problems. Guided by a routing algorithm, electronic packets hop from node to node, casting the net of real time over the globe.

New organizational structures emerge. The global twenty-four-hour office was always the hidden possibility and agenda of all programs of globalization. Now it is a reality with which practices of business and labor management must contend. From the perspective of corporate governance, the new arrangement allows work organization in two time zones to be sequentially patterned for competitive advantage—this is called the follow-the-sun approach. "Basically [when] it's night in the U.S., it's early morning here," a programmer in India explained. "At the end of their day [the Americans] just have to [compile] their problems and the changes they want us to do, and we can fix them in our normal working hours, fix them just in time, and it will be there next morning when they come to their office." The corporation's work in the United States does not stop when its employees are asleep at night, as Indian professionals keep advancing the project during their daytime. Many processing and maintenance jobs fit this model. A few American insurance companies, using this pattern, have their back-end tasks completed in India. A programmer who worked at the time in the United States to coordinate work flow between the client and his software firm in India explained, "So, at 10:00 [p.m.] here, which will be around 8:30 in Bombay, in the morning, our daily batch cycles run . . . The claims that are entered in the day [in the United States] . . . will be processed in the nightly batch cycles in Bombay. We actually have about sixty jobs running one after the other, which update the table information."

In cases like this one the time-zone difference is an asset for the corporations involved: by the time offices close in the United States and night descends, software workers in India start working on the back-end tasks during their daytime. When the CICS (computer information control system) is not in use in the United States, Indian workers can provide solutions and complete them online. When the office opens in the morning in the United States, a lot of back-end work has already been completed, thus creating a virtual twenty-four-hour office for the American client. However, this new timing of organizational flows must follow the day-and-night pattern strictly if it is to function properly, as the team in India must finish all the tasks during their daytime. "Some of the files, which [the Bombay team and U.S. team] use, are common," the programmer further explained, "so unless and until these files are closed, we cannot start our cycles. The CICS has to be down [before the Bombay team can start working]. Around 10:00 p.m. [Eastern Standard Time] the CICS goes down, no information can be entered after that, so our batch cycle [in Bombay] can run. And if the batch cycle is not successfully finished within time, or if it gets delayed due to some reason, then there will be a problem, because these people [in the United States] won't be able to enter the information [in the morning]. So, it's very critical to resolve everything [before they open their office in the United States]."

The organization of time thus again receives a major overhaul. While the principle of the timetable has been essentially negative in its conventional form, forbidding idleness with moral injunctions against wasting time, the modern conception of time has been that of a positive economy, following "the principle of a theoretically ever-growing use of time; exhaustion rather than use; it is a question of extracting, from time, ever more available moments, as if time, in its very fragmentation, were inexhaustible" (Foucault 1979, 154). To the problem of exhaustion has been added a use of time which is not available, or at least not available to a territorially co-located community. While speculative options trading may be a good example of going beyond the presently available time, my contention is simpler. Earlier, when workers went to sleep in the United States, their productive time ceased to exist. Now, technical developments associated with virtual migration make available the productive time of workers who are not part of the territorial community, using the time that was not available to them earlier.

The temporal sequencing of work across continents is not restricted to cases of third-party outsourcing. Some companies have started to follow the same model of twenty-four-hour work, for their clients in the United States and also for themselves, by dividing their work groups and assignments between India and the United States. "So this is the model we follow . . . We have a dedicated satellite," the vice-president of a company proudly claimed, "It means you are reaching a level where you are able to provide twenty-four-hour support. Time-wise, when those twenty guys are working there, we are sleeping, when we are working they are sleeping, but then they are all connected with the mother computer, the main computer, they go to the server, pick it up from where it was left off." In certain software development projects, the twenty-four-hour work schedule may allow accelerated detection of problems or a distributed daily test-and-fix cycle.

This kind of temporal integration is also common to American companies that receive an enormous number of queries for technical support. They find this model especially productive in two senses. First, tech support provided by e-mail from programmers sitting in India is obviously cheaper than support from programmers in the United States, and second, the answers to those queries can be received within twenty-four hours, given the time-zone advantage. "They give out contracts for a lot of things. So tech support was one of those," explained one programmer, who moved from India to the United States under a body-shopping arrangement and was later absorbed by a major American company as a regular employee. "Working from India was more monetarily [cost-effective]; you can hire more than double the number of people for the same amount. It also worked for India, because the various data are reported during the day [and] we can get it to them in the nighttime,

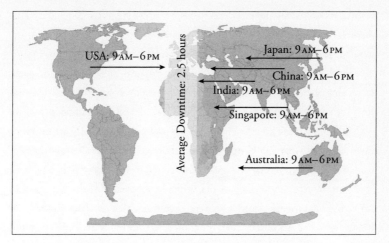

FIGURE 3. *The follow-the-sun approach to temporal integration.*

that is, nighttime here [in the United States], and people get their answers within twenty-four hours."

That technical expertise is physically located in India does not compromise the quality of work, as the software industry has developed fixed standards for governing and overseeing quality. In addition to imposing external quality standards (such as the ISO 9000 series) on general programming work—a practice that has recently been linked with deskilling and diminished job growth (Prasad 1998)—programmers in the tech support area must follow quality standards and adhere to the stipulated turnaround time for solving problems, as noted by another programmer: "We work under certain guidelines and certain principles and quality standards. All these things are documented in the contract or the agreement, so we are required to meet certain service levels. For example, the turn around time for this problem is two hours, but the other kind of problem may take four hours. It's all very well documented . . . Our effort is to meet whatever standards, whatever deliverable standards are there." A visual depiction of the twenty-four-hour office is shown in figure 3.

In this follow-the-sun approach, work hops from site to site daily. In software development, developers in California complete the day's work by passing their code to their colleagues in India who will shortly be pulling up their chairs at work. The Indian developers in their turn pass their work back to

California before diving into the rush-hour traffic in Delhi or Bangalore. This is surely not as easy as it sounds. Coordination is a complex business, requiring each party to wrap up its work in a way that it is readable and understandable by the other party, which can then quickly proceed to add value without losing the entire day deciphering what the other side did. If the virtual integration of work spans more than two sites, the problem of coordination multiplies in complexity. To overcome the problem, some software development tactics involve low coupling among relatively independent modules to be developed by different sites. Apart from regular coordination through liaisons who fly from various countries to the headquarters of the company to learn the system-level requirements and communicate them back to their colleagues at home, this form of transnational integration is heavily dependent on the governance schemes embedded in the architecture of defined interfaces and their concise semantics for the network element behaviors, along with low coupling, allowing teams that are geographically far apart to have relative independence.

However, the twenty-four-hour office model does not work in all cases. Some projects need constant interaction and lack precise specifications and standards to permit the temporal independence and neat delineation of twelve hours for each side.

Temporal Dissonance

In the event of problems and glitches, the time-zone difference hinders instant communication with the client, delaying the quick resolution of problems. Desirable as they may seem, strategies to integrate different time zones and twenty-four-hour office systems cannot universally meet all corporate needs, especially those dependent on face-to-face interactions. To overcome this problem, some companies open a branch outside the United States in the same time zone as an American site, for example in the Caribbean, to avoid higher wage costs without losing temporal proximity. As one informant who worked for a major financial enterprise described the situation: "[This company] had people working in India on projects. But . . . the time lag, time difference, [was a problem], they are sleeping and you are working, and you cannot really talk to them at the same time. [The work] was done through a [software] consulting company . . . [that] hired people in India; they worked there, and sent back some code. But it didn't work. So instead, what the consulting company came up with was that they moved them to Barbados." "So, they started working in the same time zone?" I asked. "Yes, the same time zone and same weather [as in India]," the informant responded, "And you don't have to pay them [as much as you do in the United States]; you can pay the same amount [as you do in India]."

Innovations in the governmental integration of transnational labor are constantly geared toward overcoming problems of space and time. Different models are devised for different kinds of work, costs being the constant factor in all decisions. The reframing of space and time may not always be easy or even successful, but the effort to govern and harness cheaper labor is always present. One CEO of a subsidiary of an American company in Noida, India, expressed his frustration over the time-zone difference between New Delhi and Seattle, which unlike cities on the East Coast of the United States offered no overlap with India in work hours: "In our case the problem is that it's exactly twelve and a half hours difference. So there are no common office hours. For example, if the office there started at our 4 p.m. or 5 p.m., I would be so much more happy. Because right now every meeting is an effort. On their part or on our part, both sides. Because we have to stay in office until 10 or 10:30 p.m. to have a reasonable meeting, and they need to start early, and vice versa. So that's an extra effort . . . When we worked with [our office in] Germany, it was so much easier. You know we would stay in our office till 4:00 p.m. and we would call them at 2:00 p.m., but just the U. S. West Coast, it's very hard." During daylight savings time in the United States the situation improves, but the West Coast and Delhi still do not have any temporal overlap, and this puts a heavy demand on programmers, project managers, and executives to work late at night or early in the morning so that they can find a temporal space for virtually getting together. As shown in figure 4, the Indian side must stay a couple of hours after 6 p.m. for a virtual conference with New York, and three hours more to connect with Seattle.

We can easily see that when it is time to close offices in Delhi at 6 p.m., New York is about to open its offices, and that by coming to work early in New York or leaving later in Delhi employees can create a temporal overlap to solve problems. On the West Coast, temporal distance puts more intense

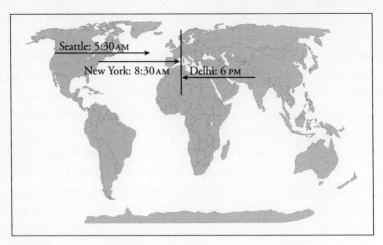

FIGURE 4.   *Temporal distance between India and the United States.*

demands on employees. Just as physical migration emerged as a problem after the rise of strict national borders, the temporal location of a place became an obstacle to overcome after the real-time integration of continents. Each new solution to global integration comes with new needs and problems. Programming work, despite a high degree of specification and standardization, still requires, like other kinds of work, meetings and communication to resolve issues of software development. The frustration of the CEO quoted above was directed not at the whole labor regime but only at problems of communication raised in his kind of work (online R&D collaboration), in which the time difference between the two places was often an impediment. He clarified: "You get advantages also. You need to decide between the model that would take advantage of the situation and the model that's a liability. In our kind of model where we are working very closely, we need to talk to a lot of people. That becomes a liability . . . That's why I said if the difference was just eight hours, it would work beautifully. Because then you are getting the advantage and you are not suffering because of the time zone difference. Because there are times when I am up at 4 a.m. [or] at midnight to attend to the phone calls, which would not happen if the time zone difference were not there."

He later made it clearer that if his American office were on the East Coast, there would be enough overlap between office hours for the system to work perfectly. What was needed was merely two hours of overlap for daily communication, so that the people in New Delhi would not have to wake up at odd hours. Clearly, systemic flexibility is often achieved by demanding immense flexibility from workers themselves, who need to adjust their waking and sleeping hours according to the demands of virtual integration.[3] The transnationally connected organizations also come into conflict with national holidays. Even when there is an overlap of hours between two sites, the countries tend to have different off-days and religious or national holidays. While the United States celebrates its Independence Day on 4 July, India observes its Independence Day on 15 August and Republic Day on 26 January. India also has many more official holidays than the United States because of its diverse religions (Hinduism, Islam, Sikhism, Buddhism, etc.) and other cultural traditions. In fact, in the late 1990s there was a discussion in the Indian Parliament about the country's large number of holidays—three times as many as the United States—and the consequent loss of productivity. The national order of things comes into conflict with the emerging real-time regime of transnational integration. The temporal dissonance is a contentious issue when setting deadlines or phone or video meetings.

In the current round of integration through information technologies, the conquest of space is simultaneously less sweeping and more drastic than earlier conquests by transport technologies. It is less sweeping because the body stays put, while symbols and signals zip across continents. On the other hand, the sheer speed of instantaneous electronic transmissions conquers space more drastically. For the first time, the obstinate resistance of space is overcome in a way that makes different times zones collide daily, as groups based in India and the United States enter into each other's time zone. As technologies of transnational governance are able to break into the local social times of people directly, they also occasion a break with their local contexts, as I discuss below.

Globally Yours: Reconfiguring the Lifeworld

At about eleven o'clock in the morning I reached the office of a major software firm in Gurgaon, a city that together with New Delhi and Noida forms the northern hub of software firms in India. It was April and the dreaded, rather early, north Indian summer had just set in. I had driven about twenty miles from New Delhi to interview the firm's senior manager. The air-conditioned interiors of the office resembled a corporate office in the United States—plush, orderly, clean, and carpeted. I always experience a culture shock at the contrast between the quiet interiors of major software firms and the outer din and disarray of Indian cities. Even from the glass opening in the door that divided the lobby from the large open office space, I could see nicely partitioned cubicles with computer monitors and phone sets. While being led to the senior manager's office, I was struck by a rather odd and curious sight: the office and all its cubicles were totally empty. During the meeting, which was cordial and informative, I could not help asking the manager about the absence of employees in this workplace. "Oh, they will start coming in at six in the evening," he responded nonchalantly. He explained that the empty part of the workplace that I saw was a call center, and workers were expected in the evening to start working during American office hours. Obviously the sparkling office space inside and the chronically unfinished construction work outside reflected not merely a contrast of two places, India and the United States; the two spaces were in different time zones. Transnational governance was fast overcoming the earlier CEO's complaint about not having enough overlap with office hours in the United States, especially the West Coast. Many firms had already adapted—by working at night—to serve their clientele in the United States during their daytime, and there was no shortage of people looking for jobs that required them to adjust and synchronize their lives with regular consumer or work hours in the United States.

Technologies of virtual mobility are increasingly made to penetrate into local times, and thereby reconfigure local contexts and the social times of people's lives. Globalization emerges as a series of different effects in different places (Guillén 2001). As physical space becomes drastically compressed by these technologies, this freshly achieved flexibility of labor supply demands certain life adjustments. People who performed nightly labor lived in two worlds. One happened during their daytime (during the major part of which they slept), marked by local languages, friendships, and relations; the other, at night, was marked by the English language as well as interactions with people living in the United States. The holidays enjoyed by the worker were those celebrated in the United States. This integration into a transnational system of labor effects a break with local mechanisms of social integration and social solidarity, by introducing what Eviatar Zerubavel (1981) calls *temporal asymmetry* as opposed to *temporal symmetry*—a temporal coordination that makes communal life possible by organizing activities in the same time frame. The importance of temporal symmetry is clear: "a most common method of punishing monks was to segregate their activities temporally from those of the rest of their community, or by having them eat their meals three hours after them, rather than together with them" (Zerubavel 1981, 65). Night work in software companies is putting workers out of phase with their own society. There is a reason why night work has another name: the graveyard shift. In this graveyard of social life (or social death?), many workers seem dissatisfied and treat their jobs as a temporary phenomenon in their lives. By placing people in another time zone, programming schemes of integration enable a systematic unhinging of people's "present" time from their concrete presence here and now, for the sake of their transpresence in another space (Virilio 1993). Spatio-temporal integration is at once spatio-temporal alienation. There is a high attrition rate among these workers. But demand for their services is growing at a high annual rate.

In the last few years, consumers in the United States have gradually become aware that when they call their bank's customer service department, the phone might ring in another continent. They may or may not know that approval for a home mortgage was conveyed to them by a person sitting in Delhi, that their medical claims were assessed by someone in Gurgaon, or that calls chasing credit-card debtors in the United States are made from Bangalore. Globalization has finally dawned on popular consciousness in a personal way. Americans are increasingly aware that that customer service agents—with friendly voices, American pseudonyms, and some training in acquiring an American accent—are telecommuting at night from India to their living rooms. Sounding "American" is important. Inauthenticity—or cultural simulation—is the very basis of authentic performance. Call-center workers in Gurgaon may tell American customers that they are calling from an American city to put these customers at ease, since their private finances could be a matter of conversation. On their cubicles are posted large nameplates with such common American names as "Victor Smith." Some call centers do not allow the workers to use their real names at all in this

FIGURE 5. *India vs. America. Cartoon by Khalil Bendib for* CorpWatch *(in Kumar and Verghese 2004). Reprinted with permission.*

Americanized space, lest they forget their American name while talking with customers.

Economics and culture merge in capital's effort to create a world after its own image. Workers watch Hollywood films to understand American diction and undergo speech therapy to sound "American" while also receiving at times, for the sake of ambience, coke and pizza on weekends. Software firms in India are now also getting part of their work force trained in American history and geography. Language plays an important part in the success of Indian software firms, as the considerable prevalence of English in India gives them an advantage over their competitors from non-English-speaking countries like China. English, a legacy of colonialism that is still used only by a small share of the population, has increased markedly since the British left India. Interestingly, colonialism was the first serious wave of transnational governance, marked by trade expansion, the administrative integration of colonies, and the spread of a few European languages, English clearly preeminent among them. The programming of postcolonial globalization also needs certain unifying mechanisms, including linguistic homogeny, to tame existing incongruities and chaos. English again comes in handy. A number of institutes opened in India to train the Indian tongue in the ways of American speech, or at least neutralize the thickness of difference. It is not the success of the night labor regime that merits attention; what is of importance is the very endeavor to erase from view the disjuncture of different worlds, different time zones, different subjectivities, languages, and accents.

With a feminist twist, the *Wall Street Journal* claims that the "revolution" brought about by call centers is not merely economic but also cultural, challenging age-old patriarchal values that prevented women from working at night: "As outsourced jobs pour into India, they are bringing much more than money to this nation of one billion. They are also creating a young, affluent class absorbing Western attitudes at the office, far from parental supervision. The independence of these twenty-somethings is helping to unravel time-honored social mores in India where young people are expected to marry someone their parents choose and live with an extended family. The idea of women working at night was unthinkable until recently" (Slater 2004). The journalistic claims of affluence as well as women's liberation must obviously be taken with a pinch of salt. I would not go so far as to describe call-center workers as affluent. Unless these young workers lived with their parents, they could only hope to rent a decent apartment at the starting salary of Rs. 8,000–10,000 in places like Delhi and Bombay. Salary raises are tightly linked with the number of telephone calls that one takes so that the targets set for one's team can be met, and the number can reach the incredibly high number of 250–300 calls a night. Still, one cannot call such practices oppressive in the regular sense of the term. The jobs are sources of income for this group of relatively young workers. Call-center work may also reflect a fascination with things American and may not be immediately perceived as oppressive or imperialistic by the workers. True, there was no desire on the part of the workers interviewed to continue in their jobs forever. Most of them left within a year. Even as a researcher, I could not spend the whole night observing work. Permanent night shifts, exceedingly high call targets, and such health problems as insomnia, weight loss, stress, and declining eyesight were some of the reasons why employees did not stay on their jobs for long.

Before one starts complaining about exploitive work conditions in India, and the absence of a level playing field for American workers, one must realize that night work is not a new or a mere transnational phenomenon. The colonization of night, to borrow a phrase from Murray Melbin (1987), has been a growing phenomenon within the United States for a long time. Recently Harriet Presser (2003), in a disturbing look at the pervasiveness of nonstandard work schedules in the United States, pointed out that two out of five employed Americans worked mostly at nonstandard times—in the evening, at night, on a rotating shift, or during the weekend. In this overlooked story about a silent, swift, and invisible social fragmentation, spouses are not together at home in the evening or at night, and parents are often not home with their children. People's integration into the twenty-four-hour economic system is also a temporal unhinging of family life. While the rhetoric of a 24/7 economy conjures up images of a fast-paced, seamlessly integrated engine that serves its consumers around the clock, the social cost of economic growth does not enter into the discussion. In virtual migration, the ever-growing subordination of the social to the economic acquires global dimensions, as this surrender of social life to the economic system can literally take place across the globe.

The intellectual left is faced with a dilemma. On the one hand, the systemic colonization of night creates a new form of inequality—work-time inequality—extending its imperial march into life's very foundations and altering circadian rhythms, which are connected with body temperature, hormone levels, and that expendable comfort—sleep. Night work may be associated with higher rates of cardiovascular disease, breast cancer, gastrointestinal disorders, miscarriage, preterm birth, and low birth weight (Boggild and Knutsson 1999; Schernhammer, Laden, Speizer, Willett, Hunter, Kawachi, and Coldtiz 2001; U.S. Congress 1991). Yet on the other hand it is difficult to assume an easy anti-capitalistic stance, because the jobs and capital generated by the software firms do help the local economy. To opt out of transnational capitalism might worsen job prospects; it might reduce the chance to have any say in projects of globalization and the direction they might take. To stand out of contemporary imaginations of world society or global membership, as discussed by James Ferguson (2002) in the context of sub-Saharan Africa, is not a real option. Indeed, it is wrong to frame the question as one of choice. Disengagement is not an option either on the part of software firms or their employees in India. The world economic system—expansionist and powerful by nature—continues to reach all pockets of the world by either favorable or unfavorable engagement. Disengagement is merely a form of unfavorable engagement. It is quite like an attempt by a student to resist the grading system by not submitting the final assignment, i.e., by not participating. But the system still engages her, if unfavorably, by giving her a failing grade. If she continues with her attempt at disengagement, she may even end up homeless with no credentials or employability, as the system reduces other support alternatives. Disengagement is impossible in another sense as well. Contrary to my slightly flawed analogy of the student, there is no single subject in the context of globalization who can exercise the choice to disengage in the first place. Saturated as our political talk may seem with language that equates nations with individuals (for example when we refer to "rogue nations"), India is not an individual subject who can disengage from globalization. The global regime has produced a new Indian transnational class whose interests are in harmony with programs of greater integration. This class in turn mobilizes through employment all local others in programs of globalization. If there are any rules still lingering from earlier times, any vestiges of the national order in conflict with the new global regime of labor, they are removed in favor of a more productive, competitive, and integrated system.

Some old rules in India are being erased to make way for the new ones. In April 2000 the governor of Tamil Nadu exempted the software industries in the state from the chapter II provisions of the Tamil Nadu Shops and Establishments Act of 1947. In effect, the rule on opening and closing hours of the shop would no longer apply to software outfits. Local restrictions designed to protect the social world from the encroachments of night work must yield to the new global labor regime. National legislation must be brought in line with global programming schemes. The Factories Act of 1948 is in for an overhaul. The act stated that no woman shall be required to or allowed to work in any factory except between the hours of 6 a.m. and 7 p.m., with the proviso that the hours may be varied as long as no woman works between 10 p.m. and 5 a.m. The Factories (Amendment) Bill 2003 seeks to remove this restriction imposed by section 66 of the Factories Act of 1948 on women's night employment. To allay the fears of the Central Trade Union Organisations that the "work environment in the country was not favourable for night work of women" and that there was a danger of harassment and exploitation, the bill allows "employment of women workers between 7 p.m. and 6 a.m. only if the occupiers of the factories make adequate safeguards as regards occupational safety and health, equal opportunity for women workers, adequate protection of their dignity, honour and safety and their transportation from the factory premises to the nearest point of residence" (Factories (Amendment) Bill 2003). The bill also mentions that "many Women Organisations have filed Writ Petitions in the various High Courts seeking directions for amending the Act to provide for night work by women on the ground that the existing provisions of the Act are discriminatory." Women in India are finally gaining the "freedom" to work at night.

The adjustment to a global labor order was begun earlier by the labor ministry itself. In a statement to the International Labour Organisation (ILO), it provided the rationale behind lifting the ban on the night shift: "Ministry of commerce has sent a proposal to the ministry of Labour that the female workers should be allowed to work in the third shift in the export processing zones to stimulate India's exports. These zones are set up as enclaves, separated from the domestic tariff area by fiscal barriers. These are intended to provide an internationally competitive duty free environment for export production at low cost. By allowing women workers to work in the third shift, it will not only help to utilise the installed capacity but will also be cost effective in the competitive international market. This would also lead to increased employment opportunities for women. Ministry of commerce is also of the view that productivity and turnover of women is much higher than that of men in the field of electronics" (Sindhu 2003). In the landmark case of *R. Vasantha v. Union of India*, the High Court of Madras in 2001 ruled in favor of a woman petitioner who contended that the Factories Act, in violation of the Constitution, discriminated against women by restricting their lawful employment. The judge agreed that denying the night shift to women amounted to discrimination on the basis of sex and gender, depriving them of chances of fair employment and equal opportunity. Calling the legislation an instance of "romantic paternalism," the judge found in it traces of the stereotype that women's role should be confined primarily to the family. The law was a way to restrict women to household activities and thus for men to retain economic superiority. Similarly, the Report of the Second National Commission on Labour maintained that "on the question of night work for women there need not be any restriction on this if the number of women workers in a shift in an establishment is not less than five, and if the management is able to provide satisfactory arrangements for their transport, safety and rest after or before shift hours" (Ministry of Labour 2002).

The above is a good description of a familiar feminist dilemma. In the first half of the twentieth century, the issue of special protective legislation for women created a split within the global women's movement, as discussed by Elisabeth Prügl (1999) in the context of homework. While equal-rights feminists condemned the legislation for its discriminatory effects, union women defended it, arguing that women's working conditions were at times objectively different from those of men. In the late 1920s this led to a split of the International Alliance of Women (IAW). Although both defenders and enemies of protective legislation preferred equal employment status for women, those who favored protective legislation regarded women as actual and potential mothers, recognizing motherhood as a disadvantage in the labor market. Equal rights feminists, on the other hand, defined women as free individuals in the liberal sense and thus contested the association of womanhood with weakness and dependence.

A proper critique should perhaps not be framed in terms of women's freedom to choose their hours of work, for surely everyone must have equal opportunities. The issue might be framed instead along the lines of a struggle for an eight-hour workday—that is, not necessarily in terms of the equal distribution of misery (night work for all) but of its reduction for both genders. The critique must uncover the effects of various programming schemes that bring about greater system integration, and the ways in which concrete social and personal lives are subordinated to system imperatives. Legislative changes are important to understand, but we must also focus on how and what governance mechanisms are coded into the programming schemes of global integration. In the next chapter, I attempt to narrow my discussion by discussing only software-based programming schemes—code—along the twin dimensions of organization and integration.

CHAPTER 5

Action Scripts: Rule of the Code

> Don't let having multiple offices in multiple time zones get in the way of
> greatness. Get together in team sites and shared work spaces that allow
> you to easily collaborate within more secure, password-protected sites.
> Now you're not just a team. *You're a finely tuned machine.* —Advertisement
> for Microsoft Office, 2004

One may read the above description of virtually integrated global work
as mere commercial rhetoric typical of all advertisements, a kind of hy-
perbole that the reader and advertiser understand to be patently false but
yet play along with, in a compelling game of consumption. What could be
farther from the truth than the portrayal of work groups separated by a vast
spatio-temporal chasm and connected by tenuous telecommunications as a
"machine," let alone a "finely tuned" one? But once we scratch the surface of
literal falsity, advertisements do contain—like the Freudian lie—remarkable
truths about the world.

Describing a team of persons spread among different time zones as a *machine* highlights a situation, or at least a desire to fashion a situation, in which
persons have been so fully integrated into the work process that it is hard to
separate them from the process itself. The machine in this case is nothing but
a process so synchronized and programmed that the extra-systemic elements
of human presence are rendered ineffective. Does this point to a modern
myth about turning humans into robots? Is this a mere repetition of Charlie
Chaplin's satire in *Modern Times* of assembly line production systems that
almost transform workers into parts of the machine? Perhaps not. In fact,
the idea of "worker teams" signifies highly nonrobotic aspects of social solidarity and collaborative problem solving. Global software development, as
one manager quipped, is a "team sport." Apparently the idea is not to sup-
press the humanity of workers. On the contrary, such nonrobotic elements of

personality as motivation, competition, and cooperation must be encouraged and augmented to achieve faster and predictable outcomes. But the process also discourages and makes ineffective those elements of personality that are out of step with systemic demands. "Peopleware" may be understood as the "human side of software" (Constantine 2001). Compare the shift of the work group toward what Microsoft describes as a finely tuned machine with earlier transformations in military organization. In contrast to the conventional idea of the battlefield as a place where "troops were used as a projectile, a wall or a fortress," in the classical period "the unit—regiment, battalion, section and later, 'division'—became a sort of a *machine* with many parts, moving in relation to one another, in order to arrive at a configuration and to obtain a specific result" (Foucault 1979, 162; italics added). Clearly there is a sense in which the idea of the machine cannot be confined to hardware alone.

Any understanding of the machine must go beyond the language of hardware or tools. A hammer is both a tool and hardware, but it is not a machine unless it is part of a programming scheme, a system of input and output, designed to produce specific results. It is not surprising that the development of the digital computer should have been aided by a hypothetical computing device called the Turing machine, which was not a physical machine but an idealized mathematical construct devised by a logician, Alan M. Turing. The Turing machine reduced the logical structure of any computing device to its core components by extrapolating the essential features of information processing. It provided the basis for all subsequent digital computers, which share Turing's basic design of an input-output device (tape and reader), memory, and central processing unit (control mechanism). Thus all machines— cars or dishwashers—must possess a programming scheme to perform their sequences, quite like computer applications informed by their source code.

Is there no difference, then, between machines of the industrial age and those of the information age? If all machines possess a "program," what is so unique about what has been termed the computer revolution? To my understanding, the difference lies in what I call the linguistification of technology, which distinguishes the programmable nature of computing devices from the programmed or closed logic of earlier machines. The next chapter addresses linguistification and its effects at greater length. My purpose here is to focus on how code exercises power over work processes extending from India to the United States in a way that makes remotely located teams of workers parts of the same machine.

How can these global teams, with no single bureaucracy to organize them in a unified work space establish a tight work regimen? What managerial hierarchy does the job of integrating or coordinating work teams? These questions about the global regime of virtual migration are relevant to a larger transformation of how work is organized in general, even within the national boundary, indeed within the same organization. More and more corporations in America are experiencing the delayering and flattening of bureaucratic hierarchies. Bureaucratic power in the workplace seems less visible and repressive, prompting many scholars to view these transformations as signifying the end of vertical bureaucratic management (Kanter 1991; Piore 1996) and the rise of what Castells (1996) calls the "horizontal corporation." If power and authority relations organized around bureaucratic hierarchies are on the decline, where do we locate new relations of power presupposed in organized work, which is, as Kunda (1992) maintains, fundamentally shaped by processes of control? My answer is quite simple: code. It is code that has gained the ability to structure possible forms of work behavior with reduced dependence on human authority relations.

Current transformations of the workplace do not necessarily represent a sequential shift from bureaucratic to post-bureaucratic management but rather a layered development of new modes of power that are increasingly embedded in information systems themselves. The decline of middle management layers owes something to the expansion of code, which like a layer of middle managers can link Wal-Mart salespersons, for instance, directly to the suppliers. Microsoft's ad invokes this power of code to organize global work teams as parts of the same machine. While a typical bureaucracy distributes power through elaborate positional hierarchies, the new form of management relies on information and software systems to govern work flows by programming the possible field of action. For lack of a better term, I call this algocracy. I do not mean that social networks at work or the human element has become superfluous. They have always been there and will always be, but we must recognize that something has changed: code not only mimics human interaction and intelligence—if in a formal, crude, and often inefficient way (think of computer-generated human voices when we call banks or airlines)—it can also embed rules and regulations in the very framework of possible tasks. For example, while filling in the "fields" on a computer screen, a bank teller cannot type in the wrong part of a form, or put the address in the space for the phone number. The embedded code provides existing channels that guide actions in precise ways, pushing the negotiability of processes out of reach. The question is not whether code succeeds completely in organizing work; rather, it is whether its insertion in business practices is increasing every day.

In the emerging complex of organizational governance, code has surprisingly remained an understudied component of the workplace. To bring out the particularity of code, I distinguish among three modes of organizational governance and emphasize the salient features of each in terms of its ruling mechanism: the bureaucratic mode (rule by the office), the panoptic mode (rule by surveillance), and the algocratic mode (rule by code). Before exploring methodically the logic of algocratic forms of governance, let me begin with a brief vignette to clarify the analytical distinction among the three forms of governance.

Driving on the streets of San Francisco—or perhaps any major city in the United States—one encounters at least three distinct modes of traffic control. There is a system of traffic lights, which one can violate only at the risk of being caught by a police car hiding around the corner. This bureaucratic system of transportation works for two reasons: the integration of the law's demands into one's personality (action orientation) and the threat of penalty (action consequence). Still, one can see that neither reason fails to stop the occasional driver who jumps the red light without being caught by the police. The second mode of control is the system of traffic cameras that can potentially catch all violations because their continuous and automatic surveillance makes escape a theoretical impossibility. If employed to its full capability, the system—based purely on action consequence—can make sure that each motorist who jumps a red light receives a citation by mail, with a picture as proof. In San Francisco installed cameras are still not used for traffic violations, but one can already see the possibility of this system. There is yet a third system of traffic control that makes it impossible to make left or right turns, or even stop, except at the points foreseen by the traffic engineers, because of the way the streets are configured and paved. In this system one does not need to be chased by the police or receive a citation by mail. One can violate the law written into the architecture only at the risk of smashing one's car into a cement block. For the sake of convenience, let us call these three schemes bureaucratic, panoptic, and algocratic. This analytical distinction among the three schemes of governance does not mean that they all work to the same degree or work at all. They may all fail to work for different reasons — traffic lights may break, the license plate of a violator caught by a red-light camera may be indecipherable, a sport utility vehicle may be able to drive over a traffic-control barrier — but the distinction makes it easier to understand how the transformation of work practices depends on the development of algocratic schemes of governance. I hope this becomes clearer after a brief discussion of bureaucratic and panoptic schemes.

Bureaucratic Schemes

In modern times, the most important analysis of bureaucracy came from Max Weber (1978) in the early twentieth century. Within the framework of his ideal type of "legal-rational" authority, he systematically studied the rise of modern bureaucracy as a new form of power and governance. For Weber bureaucracy represents an "efficient" "ideal-type" apparatus characterized by an abstract regularity of the exercise of authority centered around formal rationality. It is marked by authority relations that erode old modes of trust and social hierarchies of estate (*Ständ*) and honor, replacing them with "rational techniques" of domination. Weber situates bureaucracy within his theory of power, domination, and legitimacy, in which domination is legitimized on the basis of "legal-rational rules" in contrast to "tradition" or "charisma."

One of the modes of Weber's theory construction is to formulate purified action orientations. To explain legal-rational domination, he shows how legal-rational action orientation emerged from a struggle against monarchical absolutism in Continental Europe, a struggle that denied the legitimacy of any law based on precedent rather than statute (Bendix 1960). Thus in legal-rational governance, people who occupy positions of authority cannot act as personal rulers, and the people who obey legal-rational authority are not "subjects": they are "citizens" who obey the "law" rather than the official who enforces it. Modern bureaucracy, as opposed to the earlier bureaucracies of Egypt, China, and medieval Europe, reflects the imperatives of this legal-rationality, which is "formal" and not "substantive." By "formal" Weber implies a juridical formalism, according to which the procedures of a lawsuit emerge in a peaceful contest according to fixed "rules of the game." For instance, if one cannot afford the expense of documenting a piece of information relevant to the lawsuit, one may be forced to surrender certain rights to which one is legally entitled. Purely "substantive" and ethical considerations for justice yield to the need for predictability in "formal" procedures.

The development of modern rational bureaucracy, being dependent on formal procedures, a money economy, the free market, and the expansion of administration, is characterized by written rules in a hierarchy of specialized official positions; impersonal offices clearly distinguishable from incumbents and their private life and property; and recruitment based on qualifications, and not on the personal will of the master or leader. Weber's discussion of bureaucracy is embedded in the dual context of the legal-rational mode of domination and the technical imperatives of formal rationality that require an efficient, methodical calculation and refinement of means to achieve an end. Thus according to Weber, "business management throughout rests on increasing precision, steadiness, and, above all, the speed of operations" (Weber 1978, 974). The technical imperatives of rationality such as the speed of communication create a profound pressure for "speeding up the tempo of administrative reaction toward various situations. The optimum of such reaction time is normally attained only by a strictly bureaucratic organization" (974).

Many scholars have questioned Weber's idea of the technical superiority of bureaucracy, showing how in reality bureaucracies are fraught with informal structures and the conflicting interests of subgroups. They also dispute the notion that formal rules are efficient. Bureaucratic formal rules could be dysfunctional and have unintended consequences, as the rules become ends in themselves rather than the means to ends (Merton 1949; Selznick 1980). Informal practices may be more efficient than rigid adherence to inflexible formal rules (Blau 1967), and formal rules may be employed by members of a bureaucracy to pursue their own interests in opposition to official goals (Crozier 1967). The kind of post-Weberian research pursued by these scholars, despite its stimulating moments, has misunderstood Weber's approach, reducing the wider context of the "bureaucratization" of the lifeworld to narrow concerns for organizational efficiency. As Peter Evans has cogently argued, diminished bureaucratic controls may even lead to highly predatory state structures. Indeed, successful developmental states are marked by efficient bureaucratic regimes (Evans 1995).

In fact, the question of "efficiency" as an object of analysis is itself made possible by the rise of instrumental reason, which is institutionalized in actual bureaucracies. Weber himself acknowledges that "the bureaucratic apparatus also can, and indeed does, create certain definite impediments for the discharge of business in a manner best adapted to the individuality of each case" (1978, 974–75). To say that Weber did not describe "real life" is to have an impoverished notion of the real. He appeared to be more concerned with the imperatives of formal rationality that produce a whole series of effects in the real by acting as grids for the perception and evaluation of things. To Weber, for instance, the discretionary acts of modern bureaucratic officials are vastly different from the discretionary acts in earlier forms of administration, because in modern bureaucracy even the discretionary acts require an appeal to, and evaluation of, impersonal ends; one cannot openly confess personal favors and arbitrariness (Bendix 1960). This orientation toward impersonal rules transforms the real world in significant ways. The question is not whether Weber's ideal type was accurate; rather, the question is whether there are other developments in the modern system of governance that add complexity to Weber's diagnosis. I will briefly discuss the notion of panopticism posited by Michel Foucault (1979) as another dimension of power relations in organizational life. This discussion will help distinguish the scheme of algocratic governance from both bureaucratic and panoptic forms of governance.

Panoptic Schemes

Panoptic power, in short, is governance by continuous surveillance. Foucault borrows the concept of the Panopticon from Jeremy Bentham's eighteenth-century design of prison architecture in which all the cells, arranged in a circular fashion around a central tower, were made visible from the tower top: "By the effect of backlighting, one can observe from the tower, standing precisely against the light, the small captive shadows in the cell of the periphery. They are like so many cages, so many small theatres, in which each actor is alone, perfectly individualized and constantly visible. The panoptic mechanism . . . reverses the principle of the dungeon; or rather of its three functions — to enclose, to deprive of light and to hide — it preserves only the first and eliminates the other two. Full lighting and the eye of a supervisor capture better than darkness, which ultimately protected. Visibility is a trap" (Foucault 1979, 200–201).

Foucault uses the example of the Panopticon to highlight deeper transformations in systems of power in modern societies, reflected in the tendency toward surveillance. One of the major effects of the Panopticon, Foucault further explains, was to "induce in the inmate a state of conscious and permanent visibility that assures the automatic functioning of power" (1979, 201). "In view of this, Bentham laid down the principle that power should be visible and unverifiable. Visible: the inmate will constantly have before his eyes the tall outline of the central tower from which he is spied upon. Unverifiable: the inmate must never know whether he is being looked at at any moment; but he must be sure that he may always be so."

The principles of this mode of power, according to Foucault, have spread throughout the social body, with generalized disciplinary effects. A gradual extension of panoptic mechanisms to all social realms in the last three centuries has resulted in what he calls the "disciplinary society," in which cellular structures of temporary or permanent confinement predominate. Therefore it is not surprising that "prisons resemble factories, schools, barracks, hospitals, which all resemble prisons" (Foucault 1979, 228). We can easily extend Foucault's analysis of disciplinary effects of surveillance mechanisms to contemporary life. The growing prevalence of video cameras in shops, stores, and workplaces, and their use for disciplining the street traffic, have the effects of inducing in people "a state of conscious and permanent visibility that assures the automatic functioning of power." These surveillance systems share with the Panopticon such features as asymmetric visibility: the inmate is "totally seen, without ever seeing," and at the other end of power relations, in the central tower, "one sees everything without ever being seen" (Foucault 1979, 202). In contemporary organizations, surveillance is exercised not merely through camera-like devices but also through computer technologies that record the behavior of the user for the same purpose. Combining imaging and tracking technologies with relatively invisible practices of what is called dataveillance, computers seem to have enhanced the power of surveillance.

Computer-based surveillance systems in workplace settings, even more than bureaucratic hierarchies, implement the model of invisible authority and visible workers. The new information systems can invisibly translate, record, and display the worker's behavior, making it universally visible without the managerial eye, which is now inscribed in the system itself. As Shoshana Zuboff (1988) points out, information technologies *automate* operations (that is, they replace the human body with technology to carry out similar processes) and also *informate* operations (that is, they also generate information about the operations, for example by keeping a log of every step of a process). The production of information about work behavior and productivity, containing elements of what Perrow (1986) calls "unobtrusive control," has obvious disciplinary effects on the worker. While the gaze of information systems does not pose an immediate threat of being rebuked or discovered, it is more universal, as it freezes all work activity for possible future scrutiny. Logs of labor make escape a theoretical impossibility. For instance, the defect-tracking function in software development platforms can conduct the functional test and also log the test results. Defects may be linked to specific programmers.

In addition to appropriating the function of failure detection, which is no longer subject to managerial oversight, software systems have made it difficult for the worker to escape the organizational gaze. A variety of enterprise-level software systems (such as LittleBrother) keep an ever-watchful eye on employees' Internet behavior, offering real-time monitoring in addition to generating customized reports automatically. Other devices that are hardware-based carry out similar surveillance functions. KeyKatcher, for example, a maker of a small keystroke logger that records employees' keystrokes for scrutiny, advises employers to "use the KEYKatcher to monitor employee computer usage compliance. Employees will spend less time browsing the internet and sending e-mails if they are being monitored."

Managerial enterprise is related to the exercise of control through the watch or the look—making the worker, and the work performed, more visible to the managerial eye. One early management pioneer and successful manager, Robert Owen (1771–1858), described his introduction to managing workers as follows: "I *looked* very wisely at the men in their different departments, although I really knew nothing. But by intensely observing everything, I maintained order and regularity throughout the establishment, which proceeded under the circumstances far better than I had anticipated" (Owen 1857, 31–32). The phenomenon of the look is crucial to the exercise of managerial authority. Phenomenologically, Sartre (1966) has described the look as an attempt to control the other's freedom. Being watched or being visible limits the possibility of different modes of being to a frame of reference established through existing power relations. Foucault's concept of the "gaze" (1979) carries similar import. The look or gaze employed in surveillance systems is an instrumentally interested look. It is the responsibility of authority to look at the workers, but it is also the responsibility of the workers to keep themselves in a position where they can be easily looked at. The panoptic look does not take place behind the back of social language; it carries defined expectations, scales against which one will be judged. The look distinguishes good from bad; it is important for both punishment and reward. It is therefore important for the employees to be visible, especially when they are performing well. Asymmetric visibility thus emerges as an intrinsic aspect of panoptic power.

Both bureaucratic and panoptic schemes of power derive their efficacy from what Weber would call formal rationality; that is, they transform certain "formal" aspects of governance whereby power no longer flows from persons but is more and more embedded in rules, positions, architectures, and devices. Algocratic power also uses formal rationality, or rather the pure reason of symbolic logic, to produce yet another set of effects. This is the third mode of organizational governance that I identify and examine.

Algocratic Schemes

Bureaucratic domination was exercised by making people accept the authority of impersonal rules and regulations. Technical imperatives of formal rationality have reached a point, however, where they do not require bureaucratic orientation and authority relation to the same degree. Programming technologies have gained the ability to structure possible forms of behavior without a need for orienting people toward accepting the rules. Work is increasingly controlled not by telling workers to perform a task, nor necessarily by punishing workers for their failure, but by shaping an environment in which there are no alternatives to performing the work as desired. As mentioned earlier, the fields on a computer screen can be coded to allow only certain kinds of texts or digits. Software templates provide existing channels that guide action in precise ways. This guidance suggests that authority does not need legitimacy in the same sense, because either there are no alternative routes to the permissible ones or the permissible routes are themselves programmed. There is no comparison that can be used to delegitimate authority. This is what I imply by algocracy: authority is increasingly embedded in the technology itself, or more specifically in the underlying code, rendering the hierarchical system of authority relations less useful. Thus, the following statement of Weber is in need of a revision: "Once fully established, bureaucracy is among those social structures which are the hardest to destroy . . . As an instrument of rationally organizing authority relations, bureaucracy was and is a power instrument of the first order for one who controls the bureaucratic apparatus . . . Where administration has been completely bureaucratized, the resulting system of domination is practically indestructible" (Weber 1978, 987). In view of flattening hierarchies, many argue that the indestructibility of bureaucratic structures prophesied by Weber is no longer a stable truth (Kanter 1991; Piore 1996). But one must not read Weber's ideas on bureaucracy, as I argued earlier, in conjunction with his larger claims about formal rationality, which is in fact present and well in the algocratic layer of governance.

Algocracies appear to gradually replace the early subject-object relationships, in which a superordinate as an observing subject watches over the work of a subordinate. Programming has empowered the smart machine with the ability to point out incorrect steps taken by the user, and also to suggest at times the correct method to the ignorant worker. Unlike the unlettered machines of the industrial age, the new machine has the ability to communicate commands as an authority in addition to faithfully carrying out commands of the worker. The ability of the computer to assume the role of the controlling authority—apart from being the object of work—turns the unidirectional relationship with industrial machines on its head. I identify a set of factors that allow us to talk and think about algocracy as a distinctive mode of organizational governance.

This comparison does not imply that we are dealing with separable organizational forms, for in reality they are three dimensions of governance that exist side by side in organizations. But the supremacy of a particular dimension of governance has specific effects. Algocratic governance implements flatter network-based power relations, where all are subordinated like nodes in computer networks, giving rise to what is called the "horizontal corporation." No wonder recent years have witnessed immense changes in the American workplace. As Manuel Castells (1996, 176) points out, "The main shift can be characterized as the shift from vertical bureaucracies to the horizontal corporation." A number of scholars have discussed the rise of decentralized, de-hierarchized, "post-bureaucratic" organizations, characterized by highly skilled work, a centrality of knowledge workers, and increased worker autonomy (Attewell 1992; Block 1990; Clegg 1990; Hirschhorn 1984). New flexible work systems (Osterman 1994) are said to have resulted in the empowerment and reskilling of workers, who are engaged in trimming the "fat" and flattening the rigid bureaucracies of the workplace (Heydebrand 1989; Kanter 1991; Kanter 1989). Many big corporations are chastised for still being confined in "bureauspace"—the mechanistic culture of bureaucracy (Kanter 1996). Michael Piore (1996) discerns a resurgence of small business and entrepreneurship, along with a decentralization of power and responsibility in large organizations, and claims that the contemporary emphasis on network organizations disproves the historical visions of Weber, Schumpeter, and Marx, contained in the ideas of bureaucratization and alienation. The reengineering of business organizations, especially in the United States, also seems to mark the decline of managerial positions—the epitome of bureaucratic authority—rendering whole layers of middle managers and their staffs redundant (Boyett and Conn 1991; Cappelli 1992).

The managerial revolution in the nineteenth century was an important event in the history of business enterprise. It was the time when the "visible hand" of salaried managers, according to Alfred Chandler (1977), replaced the "invisible hand" of market forces in coordinating the economy and allocating its resources, marking the change from small traditional family firms to large bureaucratic business enterprises. Simultaneously, the rise of a nonowner managerial stratum separated ownership from control, calling into question the binary class analysis of orthodox Marxist social theory (Burnham 1960; Geiger 1969; Marshall 1977). After about 1980, however, middle managers, long insulated from job insecurity, seemed highly vulnerable to job displacement. The restructuring undertaken by eighty-nine of the hundred largest corporations in the United States in the following years resulted in substantial management layoffs ("Management Layoffs" 1985). Capelli (1992) found that during the mid-1980s, after controlling for individual and industry characteristics, managers were found to be more susceptible to displacement than other workers, experiencing proportionately greater job loss from attempts to restructure and downsize organizations, and from plant closings. According to the Bureau of Labor Statistics, the number of unemployed managers in 1990 was 12 percent higher than it was in 1989 (1990). Numerous articles in both scholarly and popular literature chronicle the wholesale elimination of management layers and a shortage of comparable positions for the displaced professionals. According to a survey conducted by the American Management Association (1995), while middle managers made up only 5 to 8 percent of the American work force, they made up 18 percent of the jobs eliminated between 1988 and 1995 for which a level could be identified. According to many scholars, in contrast to the vertical gradations and specialized division of labor of industrial bureaucracies, a "two-tier" structure is emerging in which middle-level positions are eliminated (Burris 1993; Hodson 1985; Noyelle 1987).

In their role as bureaucratic authority, managers have long enjoyed the image of a group shielded from the displacements associated with economic and organizational changes. Entrepreneurs and managers have been lumped together in the same social group by virtue of their position in economic enterprise, and the common problems and experiences to which their positions expose them (problems of productivity and efficiency). Further, as controlling subjects managers have been the ones who have made layoff decisions. But the harbinger of change, the protected supervisor of the workplace, is steadily becoming a casualty of change. The displacement of middle-management positions reflects a vulnerability and a decline in their functional significance introduced by algocratic systems of governance. There is a certain dilution of managerial authority that merits attention. A vertical disintegration of corporations combined with the relative autonomization of internal units and individuals appears to question the Weberian thesis of strict office hierarchies as a defining aspect of modern organizations. In fact, it is precisely the decline of office hierarchies that makes the Weberian argument about the ascendance of formal rationality more relevant than ever.

The decreasing significance of managerial hierarchies does not imply the decline of "management" or the liberation of the worker; rather, the new structures are invested with a different form of power. The continued disintegration of vertical management may be linked with the rise of technologically coded authority—that is, algocracy. For the sake of convenience, I will explore algocratic governance along two lines—work structure and work flow—to understand its connection with vertical disintegration and horizontal integration. As work structures themselves become "templates" of organization, there is a need to rethink what we mean by organizations and work structures.

Work Structure

Organizations are above all specific cases of organization, or the structuring of work. Most research on bureaucracy has tended to focus on real organizations populated by people and bounded by walls. Against this sociological realism, Weber's original idea of the legal-rational organization of organizations got lost. By analyzing algocratic governance, I wish to get to back to the basis of organizations: the organization, or the ordering, of work. As I pointed out earlier, the basic difference between bureaucratic governance and algocratic governance is that the organization of the first revolves around impersonal, written rules that everyone must adhere to, whereas the second is based on underlying codes that do not necessarily require rule adherence, as they tend to channel work behavior along programmed logics. Let me describe how banking software is developed by programmers in India for an American bank and how this code then governs actual work behavior. A systems analyst described the development and function of the application software as follows: "Application software is . . . like banking as an application. What we do is support your daily requirements for banking applications like daily branch opening, your account handling, your money transfers, everything, the routine tasks for which there is a need to build the software. It's very routine because most rules are documented. You just have to implement those business rules into software programs." While the systems analyst does not think much of the "routine" job of translating regular banking processes into software applications, these applications do not behave exactly like their previous physical processes. They change how banking work is organized. Installed as the transnational platform of a bank's distributed computer networks, these applications turn rules and routines into algorithmic code, acquiring a certain power of structuring, for instance, how a bank teller would perform her tasks. Let us see how this kind of bank application guides and governs a bank teller's work behavior, in her own words: "You log on, do your password, then your screen opens . . . there are functions on the top, that say twenty one is a cash advance, twenty two is . . . , and it does nothing until you put in the number for the transaction you're going to do. Then there is a list of the amount—is it cash, is it check, does he want cash back . . . and [the relevant screen] pops up; if it's over a certain amount, another screen pops up and says, did you check ID. So, it's pretty basic, it takes you step by step through the transaction. It says, now give the customer this much money, and asks you if this amount is correct. And so you fill in numbers for all the sections, hit enter, it will take you to the next step. You will validate the thing you're holding—the check, the slip, the transaction—and then it asks if there is anything else you want to do for the customer. And you say yes, or no."

This example of algorithm-based structure demonstrates how the worker's subjective orientation or adherence to rules is less important than following the steps suggested by the program, which tends to disallow other ways of doing work, requiring only "saturated" skills (Aneesh 2001). Even if organizations use a graphical interface that seems to offer more choices for the worker, all choices are already programmed and nonnegotiable in way that represents a departure from the teller's earlier use of physical registers. The bureaucratic steps that the teller needed to take to make an entry into a register were first learned, memorized, and internalized; she needed to know which entry goes into which column on which register with a personal commitment to following the rule. The connection between the teller and the register was not as tight or seamless as that between parts of a "finely tuned machine." Sure, a hacker may hack into banking applications, playing a role similar to that of a nineteenth-century Luddite (although with more technological sophistication) and bringing the software back into the realm of negotiability; yet in practical life most tellers are not hackers.

Software applications of this sort are not confined to banks; their use is quite widespread in drastically different kinds of organizations, including airports, hospitals, department stores, and state institutions like departments of motor vehicles, to cite a few. Algocratic governance depends on this programmability of work. Most institutions in the United States have injected the dimension of algocratic governance into their existing bureaucratic controls. I do not suggest that old ways of performing work were somehow "better": the focus of this argument is only how algocratic governance implements a programming scheme that pushes processes of negotiability into the background.

The dominance of algocracies has not yet reached its peak. In my interviews, many systems analysts corroborated the findings of Salzman and Rosenthal (1994) that institutions prefer to replicate the previous work structure into software systems despite contentions by systems analysts that they are inefficient. This insertion of algocracies into bureaucratic work structures takes different forms. Corporate attempts to completely reengineer their organization through enterprise resource planning (ERP) systems exemplify not only an effort to avoid the inefficiencies of earlier systems but a rethinking of the very structure of organization. Just as McDonald's uses certain fixed principles in its franchises throughout the world (such as the physical arrangement of the kitchen and counter, the cooking devices, and the tasks assigned to workers), it has become possible to create templates of work organization, coded in software programs, that can be customized to a business's particular needs (despite appearances, the customizations are nothing but programmable standardizations). In a certain sense, software companies in India are in the business of selling customized organizations, complete with ready-made templates and modules for managing the supply chain, payroll, job costing, the sales force, the product life cycle, and customer relationships.

Algocracy does not merely *represent* existing organizational structures; it seems to *simulate* them; that is, a product such as Microsoft Office affects how people think of offices. It would be a mistake to think of the term "office" in the Microsoft Office suite as merely metaphorical, since this Office does contain folders, files, and databases that can fill up physical file cabinets in offices; it does contain an accounting department that can download "real" data from the banks and process it; it also has a secretary that can take dictation. Yet Microsoft Office produces couplings and structures that go beyond prior structures. Numerous customized enterprise software systems being developed by software vendors in India do not merely represent the real; they also produce the real. These simulated organizations running on silicon chips do not necessarily follow real organizations; rather, they precede them. Reality may imitate theory. But we must not fall prey to the division between the virtual and the actual, or the often discussed difference between representation and simulacrum (Baudrillard 1983). An actual thing is produced only from virtual possibilities. There must already be some general image of the Fordist assembly line production system if one is to build, recognize, and perceive one as an actual system. Thus our "real" world is always virtual-actual. It is not just that the actual world is an effect of virtual potential; each actual thing maintains its own virtual possibilities because of the ever-present possibility of new combinations. The assembly line production system, for example, can one day become a museum attraction, or a presentation slide in a classroom.

Enterprise software systems are not merely the automation of existing processes, as many software professionals themselves understand automation; they also relate in a deeper sense to an imagining of processes that do not exist yet but need to be born. Quite like models of cars and machinery designed through computer-aided design (CAD) systems, simulated models of organizational processes facilitate a controlled outcome. Elaborating upon the concept of simulation, one computer scientist stressed the various advantages of simulating expensive products: "Suppose . . . I want to build a car. There are two ways you could actually do it. You could actually build a car and see if it works. Or you could build a fake car . . . in the mind of your computer, and then ask the computer to see if it works. The second way is better because you don't waste money, buying material. If you are doing a space shuttle, for instance, they can't afford to send five space shuttles to figure out some mistakes first. So, they simulate everything inside a computer to see if it will work." Software facilitates the imagination of new car designs with the possibility of going straight from CAD to prototype tooling, bypassing standard clay models (as was done with the Toyota Sportivo). Similarly, coded templates of organization can go beyond the expression of existing structures to reflect the rise of a technology that can potentially program an imagined system of governance even before it comes into existence. Failures in implementing imagined processes will occur, but failures themselves point to a definite transformation in conceptions of control and governance. Programmability indicates governability.

Previous organizational unities experience disintegration under the governmental integration of transnational labor. If firms based in India are able to provide accounting services through shared data servers, there is less need to have an accounting department or a payroll division within organizational walls. The much discussed vertical disintegration of corporations (Castells 1996, 176) is made possible through the semiotic integration brought about by programming languages, giving rise to horizontally integrated processes across the globe. The practice of software development itself is affected by this transformation, leading to horizontal, multisite, multicountry distributed development approaches. *Distributed development* is a practice that allows a project's development resources — including development tools, hardware, middleware, and the development staff — to be distributed among globally dispersed development centers, as discussed in chapter 4. Yet distributed work is more than work distributed geographically: the process of distribution also involves dividing and organizing work content among different teams of developers. Indeed, distributed software projects spanning multiple development locations are becoming the norm rather than the exception.

Distributed Structure: Algocratically Defined Work Space

Distributed software development tends to depend on software platforms that algocratically integrate work processes between India and the United States using such tools and development environments as BSCW, MetaEDIT+, ClearCase, MultiSite, and more general-purpose technologies like Corba. Algocratic controls in globally accessible software platforms may consist of a number of components: Unified Modeling Language (UML), which offers a unified graphical approach to follow the logical structure of the project; version control, which prevents more than one person from making changes to a file at a time, guaranteeing that everyone has access to the correct file version; defect tracking and testing; and various communication tools such as discussion boards and file annotation. With multisite data replication and a problem-tracking tool shared by all teams, these software platforms let each team work in relative independence while still providing visibility to changes from other teams. The web integration of the problem-tracking tool and shared library allow a lightweight interface with full visibility.

As miscommunication is a common problem plaguing distributed work, the above components of software project management enforce a common work process and a common view of the project. The common work view does not necessarily mean centralized development. Recent innovations in global software development—commonly called modular and component-based development—suggest the contrary. Many collaborative projects undertaken by Indian companies enjoy low coupling among clusters, to allow each team to run independently of any other team as well as the original architects of the project. Each team could run in loose synchrony with the other teams, meeting them at the cluster integration points. For some projects, the teams are in charge of complete subsystems into which the source code of large software products is typically organized according to major function (database, user interface, and so on), reducing communication problems between development centers. Global software development follows new innovations in programming designs. For instance, eXtremeProgramming (xp) and Component-Oriented Rapid Development (cord) allow processes to happen in parallel cycles rather than in a sequential fashion. xp replaces the sequential steps of the waterfall model found in most object-oriented software engineering approaches with an extremely large number of parallel steps, including analysis, design, implementation, and testing. Horizontal clusters of a divided system are developed in parallel and integrated weekly, instead of in one final "big bang." By combining parallelism with the ability to adjust the size of components, one can run global software projects in multiple sites at the same time. The components, like JavaBeans, are ready-made, platform-independent, programmed, and reusable, like car parts that can be assembled in many configurations.

When the development is occurring in a parallel, not sequential, fashion, it becomes highly important to synchronize changes and ascertain the latest version in each cycle. Version control systems such as Continuous Change Management Suite, Visual SourceSafe, and ClearCase perform this task. Version control systems may operate over a set of source code files, ensuring that the smallest change, or delta, to the program text (such as the deletion or addition of a single line of code) is tracked to synchronize the entire development with the latest version. Deltas are usually computed by a file-differencing algorithm, invoked by the version control system, which compares an older version of a file with the current version. Included with every delta is information such as a short description of the delta, the time it was made, and the person making it. Compare this system with a bureaucratic system in which a file is moved between hierarchies in its original, paper form, containing the initials of staff members who note the date and describe the changes made. In this system duplicates were carbon copies, easily distinguishable from the original. In the age of digital globalization, there is no one to carry the file across the continents, and digital copies, containing the same code, are equally original. The control is no longer exercised through the physicality of paper or initials made with physical ink; instead, the underlying structure is algocratically shaped in a way that does not allow older versions to pass as newer ones.

Algocratic governance structures have given rise to vendors specializing in providing staff from different corners of the world to corporations that agree to use their platform code. I reproduce the statement of one such company: "[We offer] a unique solution that combines the benefits of contingent staffing with virtual access to a global workforce. Using [our] technology to break the geographic constraints of traditional staffing, companies can now deploy remotely located knowledge workers in a task-based environment. In other words, [our] system enables customers to define their work as tasks that can then be dynamically assigned to a global network of virtual knowledge workers."

Clearly, algocratic systems help in integrating spatially dispersed workers and work sites. Different models of distributed development are easily identifiable in India and the United States, ranging from separate teams of independent companies to single teams of legally related companies. A distributed environment also depends on the cloning of data and software platforms, which enables workers at each site to work against a local server rather than having to reach across a wide area network for access to data that may result in performance problems or have side effects that compromise the reliability of a system. A cloned data model frees up an organization's network bandwidth, which is then used only to transfer synchronization packets from site to site rather than to shoulder the load of network traffic created by remotely located clients. Synchronization capabilities enable each clone to be updated with the changes—and only the changes—that have occurred at every other remote site since the last synchronization.

General Architecture of Distributed Systems

Multi-sided software development through virtual migration is part of a larger and more general development: the distributed network. Dating back to postwar efforts by the U.S. Department of Defense, the distributed network is most often associated with Paul Baran of the RAND Corporation, whose research was sponsored by the U.S. Air Force in the 1960s. Baran emphasized the "development of 'heuristic routing' doctrines that seek 'perfect switching;' i.e., those able to find 'best' surviving paths in a heavily damaged network. The discussion [was] restricted to those systems using 'locally' implemented switching rules, and which [did] not need a single, highly critical, control center" (Baran 1964). He was responding to an ominous concern that none of the existing structures, including the long-distance telephone plant and the basic military command and control network, would survive a nuclear attack. Once centralized switching facilities were destroyed by rival weapons, the remaining, undamaged links would serve no purpose. Therefore, Baran envisioned a distributed system without centralized switches that could operate even if many of its links and switching nodes had been destroyed. Figure 6 illustrates a simplified version of the network structures envisioned by Baran (1964).

The distributed network of unstaffed nodes would act as switches, using the shortest path to send data through available nodes to its destination. Baran also developed the idea of splitting data into message blocks before sending them out across the network. Each block would be independently routed, and all the blocks would be rejoined into a whole when they were

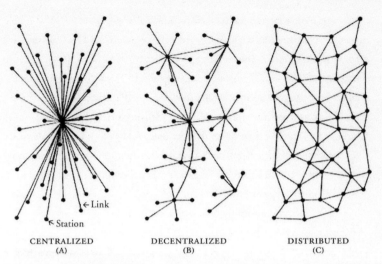

← Link

← Station

CENTRALIZED
(A)

DECENTRALIZED
(B)

DISTRIBUTED
(C)

FIGURE 6. *Network structures.*

received at their destination. Donald Davies, a British researcher, separately developed a similar system, but he used the term "packets" rather then "message blocks," and his term is the one now used. This method of packet switching is a swift store-and-forward design. On receiving a packet, a node stores it briefly and forwards it to the next node after calculating the best route to its destination. In the event of a problem with a node (for example if it has been destroyed in an attack), packets are simply routed around it. To extend Baran's insight, we might define the key characteristics of distributed networks to include failure independence (each component can fail independently while other computers keep running); the heterogeneity of components (different computer hardware; networks; operating systems; programming languages); openness, which allows components to be added or replaced (end-to-end logic); failure handling (designing for the consequences of possible failures); transparency; concurrency; resource sharing; security; and scalability (the ability to work well when the number of users increases). Some examples of a distributed network are the Internet (a large distributed system that encompasses the web, ftp, and several LANs); intranets (portions of the Internet chalked out for internal purposes by organizations); mobile or nomadic computing (using handhelds and other mobile devices); and ubiquitous computing.[1]

One may wonder about the relationship, if any, between the idea of distributed network and algocracy. In fact, code governs all layers of distributed networks: applications, services, middleware, the operating system, and computer and network hardware. Code defines the path (how messages are divided into packets, and then how they are routed), structure (how different elements of work are structured, which depends on the application), and interface (how workers interact with the screen and which access is allowed to which workers). Internet protocols that govern distributed communication are simple examples of this rule of the code. These protocols form a set of programming schemes generally called the middleware, which is a layer of code that provides a programming abstraction while masking the heterogeneity of the underlying networks, hardware, operating systems, and programming languages. Middleware is that part of the algocratic field which provides a uniform computational model for use by the programmers of servers and distributed applications.

Distributed networks have an interesting characteristic peculiar to them: components on a computer network coordinate their actions only by passing messages according to the rules set by algorithms. The concurrent components of distributed systems lack a global clock. They do not synchronize different elements of work in accordance with a single time frame. As there is no single correct time, their synchronization only means the synchronization of packets achieved by passing messages in an algocratically defined field of action.

Consider how code governs the routing of information. Routing is a function required in all global networks, except in Local Area Networks (LANs) that provide direct connections between all pairs of attached hosts. With adaptive routing, code periodically reevaluates the best route for communication between two points in the network, taking into account the current traffic in the network and any fault like broken connections or routers. Unless the source node and destination node are on the same LAN, the packet must be transmitted in a series of hops, passing through router nodes. The determination of routes for the transmission of packets to their destinations is the responsibility of a routing algorithm, implemented by a program in the network layer at each node. A routing algorithm performs two tasks: first, it makes decisions that determine the route taken by each packet as it travels through the network; second, it must dynamically update its knowledge of the network based on traffic monitoring and the detection of configuration changes or failures. This routing follows the basic principles of packet switching, which enables a store-and-forward network. Instead of making and breaking live connections to build circuits (circuit switching), a store-and-forward network merely forwards packets from their source to their destination. The postal system is a store-and-forward network for letters, with processing done by humans or machines at sorting offices. But data packets in a computer network can be stored and processed at the nodes fast enough to give the illusion of instantaneous transmission. For instance, a transmission, coded as S or F, takes anything from a few tens of microseconds to a few milliseconds to switch a packet through each network node, depending on the packet size, hardware speeds, and the quantity of other traffic. Frame relay overcomes this problem of delay by switching small packets, called frames, on the fly. The switching nodes (special-purpose parallel digital processes) direct the frames based on an examination of their first few bits; frames as a whole are not stored at nodes but pass them as short streams of bits (as in ATM technology).

There are various architectures that inform distributed systems whether employed in the global labor regime or in collaboration across the street. Two examples are well known: the client-server model and peer processes. In an algocratic field of action, clients and servers are not necessarily computers but rather code-governed processes. The server is in fact only a running program (a process) on a networked computer that accepts requests from programs known as clients running on other computers. The same computer can be both a server and a client, depending on which code is invoked. For example, a search engine is both a server and a client. Like a client it sends programs called web crawlers requesting web servers for information throughout the Internet, while providing search results to its own clients who are looking for information. There are many variations on the client-server model. Mobile Code allows java applets to be downloaded locally from the server before they run, offering better interactive response. Mobile Agents are programs (including both code and data) that travel from one computer to another in a network carrying out a task on someone's behalf, such as collecting information and eventually returning with the results. Another example is Thin

Client, a software layer that supports a window-based user interface on a computer local to the user while executing application programs on a remote computer. This architecture has the same low management and hardware costs as the network computer scheme, but instead of downloading the code of applications into the user's computer it runs them on a computer server — a powerful computer that has the capacity to run large numbers of applications simultaneously.

Peer processes follow a different architecture. They eliminate server processes, reducing interprocess communication delays for access to local objects. Consider distributed "whiteboard" applications that allow users on several computers to view and interactively modify a picture that they share. Many peer-to-peer file sharing programs, like KaZaa or Gnutella, also follow this architecture of a network without a center. There are no central servers to which various computers connect. Code handles the task of coordination among nodes.

As I discussed earlier, network transmissions are themselves coded with rules. But how do we conceive of an organizational space that may exist on such distributed networks? Where are the walls of these organizations? How are the organizational walls of a firm that exists at the same time in India and the United States closed off? First, an organizational space that spans continents must clearly be virtual in nature; so too its walls. Most intranets — virtual organizational spaces — are protected by firewalls, which like virtual algocratic walls prevent unauthorized messages from leaving or entering the system. Algocracies employ a variety of network codes that govern work flows according to underlying schemes, constituting a complex of techniques for control and access: electronic firewalls, gateways, packet filters, and proxy servers. Firewalls, for example, can examine each message entering or leaving the network, and block those that do not meet the specified security criteria. Firewalls can be implemented in hardware, software, or both. Similarly, packet filters can look at each packet entering or leaving the network, and accept or reject it based on user-defined codes. Evidently the security provided by these walls, quite like that provided by physical walls, may be compromised by various means, including viruses and hacking, but that is beside the point. Algocratic governance is itself a combination of all such techniques, including network codes with electronic protocols, coordination, and architecture that aid human nodal points with data servers. Internet-based group-ware packages integrate standard desktop applications to let organizations build far-flung project teams and transcend the need for coordination and integration through managerial layers.

One of the important roles of management layers in bureaucracies, especially middle management, is to use intra- and interdivisional communication to promote coordination and integration and achieve organizational goals. As Chandler and Hikino (1990) explain, in modern multi-unit bureaucracies, which have factories, sales and purchasing offices, and research laboratories, managerial layers have been responsible for coordinating and integrating the flow of work within and among units. Each unit has its own set of lower-level managers, whose activities are monitored and coordinated by middle-level managers, operating at multi-unit levels. The middle managers in turn are monitored and coordinated by top-level executives. Algocratic templates of work flow seem to appropriate this middle management role, enabling information networks to provide an immediate and safe passage between units in the process of production and distribution, without the need of an intermediary. In many companies, factory workers can schedule and coordinate their own production, as they have direct data links to major retailers, so they may get sales data before their better-paid senior managers do (Kanter 1989). Such direct work flows are possible for the transnational organization of work as well. Indian software companies have developed network-based information systems, facilitating the generation of purchase orders, status monitoring, and delivery of goods for companies like the Gap that are directly connected with their globally scattered vendors. By computer networks I do not mean network forms of organizations that require a high degree of mutual knowledge and trust—as discussed, for example, by Walter Powell (1990). Rather, my analysis is based on code-based interaction within and among firms. For example, a purchase order application installed on the machines of buyers and suppliers creates a code-based network that makes work progress and the status of orders instantly available on everyone's screens in the network, connecting all teams like a finely tuned machine.

Bureaucracy has been intimately related to the problem of managing information and records concerning different units in the process of production. Record keeping has been a major technology of power (Boyes-Watson 1995), allowing better managerial control over the work process. Assisted by mass storage devices and eternal memory, algocracies act as systems of permanent registration, coding all information in digital formats, complete with electronic management and control. This real-time data storage application means that the data is collected and entered into the system once and everyone can look at the same thing simultaneously, though with different degrees of authorization to manipulate the data. The result is that information now flows directly from lower-level units to top management, with a reduced need for middle managers. The findings of many studies that computerization is correlated with fewer hierarchical levels and a two-tier occupational structure (Hodson 1985; Noyelle 1987; Smith 1993; Wellman, Salaff, Dimitrova, Garton, Gulia, and Haythornthwaite 1996) do not necessarily mean looser control or the absence of authority. They point rather to a transformation in systems of governance, a partial migration to programmable governance based on the rule of algorithms, of signs and codes.

The ability of organizations to employ workers not located within the walls of their organization does not mean that the centralized structures of organizations will suddenly disappear. As corporations still must abide by national regulatory laws, their structures will continue to have the conventional appearance of firms located in specific national spaces, with definite physical addresses and staff. Moreover, the ascendancy of algocratic schemes does not mean that bureaucratic schemes have been completely abandoned. One key characteristic of bureaucracy stressed by Weber—documentation—is highly important for global collaborative development. Software firms are locked in a constant battle with programmers' well-known resistance to documentation. Programmers are required to work with technical writers to produce release notes, installation procedures, and other user documentation. In addition to documenting the various artifacts, global software development also requires the discipline of updating and revising the documentation to clarify assumptions and dispel ambiguity. Further, to support maintainability at a later date, documentation must show which instruments various teams are using and working on. In some cases, the release notes are the formal documentation for the subsystems, written as HTML pages and posted online so that all internal programmers can see them. Documentation also consists of commonly defined milestones and clear entry and exit criteria. Parallelism in global software development, combined with a lack of informal communication, volatile requirements, incompatible data formats, unstable specifications, and different versions of the same tools, makes good documentation a necessity.

Algocratic integration is certainly not as smooth, seamless, and trouble-free as it may sound. But the expansion of an algocratic regime points to a certain blurring of enterprise boundaries within the existing framework. Organizations are increasingly able to externalize their sales, distribution, manufacturing, information systems, payroll, and legal management. The explosion of practices commonly described in such economistic terms as subcontracting and outsourcing signals a business-to-business integration established through the rule of code. If customers call their bank in the United States and the phone rings at a firm in India that can provide various services by directly accessing the customers' accounts in real time by using data servers, this signifies the development of a governance structure that extends beyond the unitary model of organizations registered with the state. If travelers are automatically given the option of renting a car from a rental company on the web site of an airline after purchasing an air ticket in a single credit card transaction, this organizational integration is clearly a result of code-based governance, or more precisely the simple object access protocol (SOAP) toolkit, which allows work flows not only within an organization but also between separate firms.

Organizational forms have never been confined to organizations alone. Bureaucratic and panoptic forms of governance are in symbiotic relationship with general social structures as well. Bureaucracy in the workplace reminds us of the bureaucratization of social life, with timetables, time management, and "appointments" with friends and family a quotidian reality. Panoptic governance has seeped into our streets, homes, and shops with the advent of surveillance devices used by the consumer, police, and military alike. Consider DARPA's plans to award a three-year contract for up to $12 million to develop, for the Pentagon, a technology called Combat Zones That See (CTS). The system would "produce video understanding algorithms embedded in surveillance systems for automatically monitoring video feeds [from a large numbers of cameras] to generate, for the first time, the reconnaissance, surveillance and targeting information needed to provide close-in, continuous, always-on support for military operations in urban terrain" (Defense Advanced Research Projects Agency 2004). It is presumed that the system will be capable of automatically identifying vehicles by size, color, shape, and license tag, or drivers and passengers by face, in a foreign city. It is obvious that such a system will have nonmilitary uses as well. Technologies are open-ended and can always migrate into other areas. At times, the same device may be assigned different purposes. While the discovery of a hidden camera in the women's toilet at Cambridge University (BBC 2001) was considered an invasion of privacy, closed-circuit television cameras installed by a school in its toilets to stop smoking and graffiti (BBC 1999) could be perceived as an attempt to create a "safe" environment for younger children. With the growing tendency toward surveillance in everyday life, the uncertain response to it among many reflects the common tendency to focus on the tradeoff of privacy versus security, while ignoring the larger dimension of a social setup that continuously reduces spaces for negotiation.

Algocracy too extends beyond organizations. The rule of code determines, in a logical, step-by-step approach, which choices a person operating an ATM must make and which actions he or she may take, and the code behind an Internet transaction similarly channels behavior along specific directions. Lawrence Lessig (1999; 2001) has pointed out how the code underlying cyberspace is capable of providing perfect regulation, taking over to a certain degree the functions of copyright law, and thus limiting the web's promise as a commons. Programming has emerged as a form of power that structures possible forms of action in a way that is analytically different from bureaucratic and surveillance systems. The promised introduction of XML-based web services also points to a direction where software will no longer be sold as a "thing" to be purchased but as "code" that will provide various services to the user on demand. This transition is talked about among programmers as a shift from "products" to "productized services." Corporations that plan to provide such services expect greater profits, as well as greater control over the whole process through the algocratization of services and commodities.

The analytical separation of bureaucratic, panoptic, and algocratic forms of governance should in no manner suggest that the three forms cannot be combined in different configurations. Let's look at the technology of radio frequency identification (RFID) tags, which combines both panoptic and algocratic forms of governance. Radio frequency identification employs a tag reader (a low-powered radio transmitter) to set up an electromagnetic field, along with a passive transponder—say, a chip on the back of a shirt—that draws enough power from the RF signal to send back a hard-coded ID number as far away as a hundred feet. The reader decodes the reply, checks the store database, and registers the information. It is a form of code reading that makes things *visible*. Wal-Mart is deploying RFID tags with embedded electronic product codes (EPC) for tracking and identifying items at the individual crate and pallet level in its supply chain. This technology is expected to enhance inventory management and reduce shoplifting. The combination of code and visibility has appeal in many other potential applications, such as monitoring the allocation of beds in a hospital and the distribution of nurses (who can wear RFID tags).

Two objections may be raised against my account of algocracy. First, the architect always precedes the architecture. Before algocratic programming schemes can govern work processes, some human agent must program them in the first place. The programmer must precede the program. Second, what is so new about programmed systems of governance that make work processes nonnegotiable? It has long been pointed out by scholars (Edwards 1979; March and Simon 1958) that both technical and decisional controls may be exercised by making the basic premise uncontestable.

The first issue is basically the question of technological determinism, which one may read in the thesis of algocracy. Sociologists of science and technology (Bijker, Hughes, and Pinch 1987; Bijker and Law 1992; MacKenzie and Wajcman 1999) have long explained how technologies are themselves shaped by the social groups involved in their initial design and production. Once the technologies are shaped, one still cannot predict how they will be adopted and appropriated after their initial design, or what "affordances" that a technology permits, both realized and unrealized. Technology is not a superhuman agency, an agency smarter or less fallible than humans; rather, it is a human activity, a golem, a "bumbling giant," not evil but "a little daft," a "lumbering fool who knows neither his own strength nor the extent of his clumsiness and ignorance . . . Science is not to be blamed for its mistakes;

they are our mistakes. A golem cannot be blamed if it is doing its best. But we must not expect too much" (Collins and Pinch 1993, 2; 1998).

I agree that algocracy is shaped by all the stakeholders, including investors, managers, and programmers. In global software development, for instance, people first meet and work on the models as a group around a whiteboard. Often they will develop several models at once—perhaps several use cases along with some screen sketches, some sequence diagrams, and a class diagram. But algocratic systems also go beyond the immediate stakeholders. Paul Edwards (1996) has shown how the general development of computer technologies and scientific disciplines, such as artificial intelligence in the twentieth century, followed a specific pattern of military interest and support. Moreover, code is a kind of language—a programming language, to be precise. Like language, the social in algocracies precedes the technical. As free-floating programming schemes, algocracies are imbued with social ideas of control as well as formal logic, tracing their roots to the imperatives of capital and code. Algocracies can possess inherent political qualities, and quite like other technologies they can embody specific forms of power and public order. As Langdon Winner (1986) pointed out, a technological choice is simultaneously a choice for a social setup. Algocracies surely do not descend from heaven; yet once in place, they do structure reality, like the paved structure of San Francisco streets, in a way that exhibits significant social implications. They produce a social space that must conform to the virtual scheme present in the architectural design. For example, institutions of the "free market" do not happen in a social vacuum: I would go further, and document how the abstract and inherently flawed theory of the free market has social consequences that are peculiar to it. The resulting order, over time, tends to become natural and obvious. And as noted above, algocracies, like any other technology, often migrate from the original intent of the architect. Unlike the paved street they are reprogrammable, but they are also capable of providing greater control precisely because of their symbolic flexibility. It is also possible that programmers may code governance structures into the architecture, but at the same time they are not necessarily the authors of the programming languages they use, or of mathematical logic that can be traced back to the Enlightenment.

The absence of human agents in the algocratization thesis is deliberate, for the thesis is about a particular mode of the exercise of power. By extending the Weberian thesis that in a bureaucracy persons are replaced by positions in matters of governance, one may argue that algocratization reduces the power of positions by implementing finely tuned action scripts, almost invariably decentering the authority from the body of a person for the immediate exercise of power. This is not to deny that programming is done by someone; in fact my choice of the term "programming schemes" implies that programming is not a static, fixed object but a continuous temporal act, like the planning conducted by someone. Yet programming also becomes fixed and congealed as a scheme, defining and channeling possible action. For this kind of analysis, it is not as important to know "who" exactly programmed a particular scheme. Following the linguistic turn in philosophy, I would like to avoid the question of subject or individual consciousness. Consciousness is always already infiltrated with the world, its norms, values, and styles of thinking. Even biologically, with the gradual hard-wiring of neural networks in infancy under the influence of social and physical environments, the idea of consciousness as pure agency appears merely metaphysical. Consequently, the concept of algocracy does not refer to the consciousness—obscure or obvious—of the manager or worker or investor, nor does it refer governance to the will of the work designers. The thesis of algocracy is not geared toward unearthing the hidden *intent* of work design, an intent that always goes beyond what is actually designed. Instead, algocracy allows us to analyze the design itself and mark its actual and possible social effects.

Algocratization, quite like bureaucratization, must be seen as part of a larger discursive formation, which makes it pointless to look for the specific authors of programming schemes. Programming, as a form of power, is part of this widespread discursive formation under which all processes are understood in terms of code. The everyday understanding of self, subjectivity, and psychology is beset with the terminology of code and communication, as a result of which the mind or brain emerges as an information processor or set of programs, and memory becomes a mechanism for the retrieval of stored data (Edwards 1996; Lakoff and Johnson 1980; Turkle 1988). It is not merely self and labor that emerge as problems of coding; our existence itself is understood in terms of code—genetic code. The biological realm becomes a system of information transmitted through DNA strands; the human genome appears as a book of life, as "the *language* in which God created life," as Bill Clinton (2001) put it. The extensive use of code, language, and information is part of a different discursive space on which it has become possible to inscribe labor and life. Thus coding emerges as an a priori method of ordering a confused and chaotic world, its planes and boundaries, a veiled scheme that determines the way things confront one another. It is no mere accident that programming and coding are intrinsic to an emerging labor order, producing different relations of power, authority, and governance. The rule of code or algocracy thus adds a third dimension to the already existing bureaucratic and panoptic systems of governance.

This brings us to the second objection regarding the novelty of the thesis. Algocracies may easily be compared with Richard Edwards's argument (1979) that implementing technical controls has long been a universal method to transfer control from workers to employers. On the assembly line, the classic example, the machinery itself directs the labor process and sets the pace. Similarly, Herbert Simon (1997) has pointed out how managers are able to exercise control by shaping the very premises of decision making by subordinates. By creating structures that affect what and whom subordinates know, managers are much more likely to have subordinates make decisions that are in the best interests of the organization. Yet another example would be the speed bump, or sleeping cop, of Bruno Latour, which despite being nonhuman contains within it a "motive," structuring reality in a way that delegates a social rule to a device. Agreeing with all the above accounts, I do not intend my argument to be read as something completely new. Instead I would ask the reader to consider the thesis of algocratization in terms not only of its local uses — providing technical controls in an organization — but also of a larger discursive transformation, as I have discussed above. The next chapter deals in greater detail with the theme of code as more than a tool of technical control in a narrow sense, as a language with money-like liquidity. That discussion should distinguish algocracy a little more from existing accounts of governance.

CHAPTER 6

Code as Money

Money is like love . . . Once you have some, it can go on multiply-
ing, each part dividing itself, doubling and doubling like the cells of
an embryo. —Hilary Mantel (2000)

Remember, that money is of the prolific, generating nature. Money can
beget money, and its offspring can beget more. —Benjamin Franklin

The generative nature of money, especially in the context of global capital,
is well known. Money never sleeps. Its ceaseless expansion or contraction,
due to mechanisms of investment, interest, and inflation, are understandable. Reinvested, it may produce more of itself. Uninvested, it may shrink in
value. But it is not this productive, economic character of money that I wish
to investigate. Money is also a form of code, sign, or language, at least in its
modern role as all-purpose avatar; and thus it can be multiplied literally by
generating more of the signs, indeed by simply increasing the money supply.

Money came to be created, generated, and multiplied at first when bank-
ers discovered that they could make loans merely by issuing promises to pay,
or banknotes, to borrowers. In this fashion, banks began to produce money.
More notes could be issued than the gold and silver on hand for two reasons:
first, notes were mere "signs" or "numbers" written on pieces of paper, and
thus available in plenty in contrast to the limited supply of gold; second, only
a small portion of the total notes outstanding would be presented for payment at one time and thus needed to be settled. Reserves of metallic money
were required only to cover that portion. We can compare banknotes with
today's transaction deposits. When I deposit $1,000 into a bank, a simple
book entry is made in my checking account. The bank in turn can loan $900
to someone else, keeping available a required ratio of currency reserve (perhaps $100) to make a payment on demand. This allows the borrower to *spend*

$900 by writing checks, in effect printing money. Those checks get deposited in other banks (the borrower's payees' banks), and become in turn available for further loans (say, $810 at the second stage). True, money cannot grow indiscriminately. But the process may continue through many more stages, in increasingly smaller increments, until the entire $1,000 of reserves has been covered by deposit expansion.

I do not intend here to explain the basics of money and banking explained in economics textbooks. Instead, I want to draw attention to the algebra of modern money, which multiplies as code by unhinging itself from physical forms. This liquefaction of commodity money into a system of legible signs bears an important resemblance to software code. One may ask why this comparison is important for the programming of globalization. The answer is simple. Money and code are the media without which various global integrations cannot take place. While the importance of money is clear in global exchanges, especially in the context of fully convertible currencies, the significance of code is less frequently discussed. Let me make the comparison between money and code along three dimensions: liquidity, language, and governance.

Liquidity

The term "liquidity" in economics refers to the ease of convertibility of any asset into money. Cash is considered the most liquid form of asset. In fact, the very definition of money revolves around the idea of liquidity. Different concepts of money—M1, M2, M3[1]—in economics are defined according to degrees of liquidity. But cash, the most liquid variety of money, in itself has no value: it is a mere number, printed on a piece of paper and backed only by social promises. But being a number, a sign, and thus easy to carry, it also becomes the easiest means of exchange, allowing commodities to float in a liquid medium. Modern all-purpose money thus becomes the integrative universal medium that allows all products and services to find common ground for exchange. In many respects, programming code—as an integrative power—resembles money. Code, like money, is a universal medium, a symbolic system, and a tool for standardization, system integration, and governance. "Money of the world serves as the universal medium of payment, as the universal means of purchasing, and as the universally recognised embodiment of all wealth," Marx claims. "Everything becomes saleable and buyable . . . Just as every qualitative difference between commodities is extinguished in money, so money, on its side, like the radical leveller that it is, does away with all distinctions" (Marx 1998, 191, 207).

To economic sociologists, the argument that money "does away with all distinctions" may appear exaggerated. For instance, Viviana Zelizer (1994, 24) argues that premodern, nonuniversal moneys—shells, coins, brass rods, or stones—are in many respects similar to modern money. "How else do we distinguish a bribe from a tribute or an allowance, a wage from an honorarium, or an allowance from a salary? How do we identify ransoms, bonuses, tips, damages, or premiums?" Zelizer's argument confuses money with the social contexts of exchange, however. For example, the term "ransom" is not denotative merely of money but rather of a forced exchange obtained by a threat between parties. Still, it is precisely the universality of the money medium that makes it possible for the ransom money to be used for any other purpose. So there is not a great deal wrong with the classical characterization of modern money. Yet classical theory does fail to conceive of money as a nonsocial entity. Paper currency, as I said earlier, is only a social promise, indeed an institutional promise anchored in property and contract law; it may break down with the breakdown of social institutions, as witnessed during the Great Depression of the 1930s or the Asian financial crisis of the late 1990s. If one employs the insights of Karl Polanyi (1957), the historicity and institutional foundations of money are easily understandable. Money in its very foundation is infused with specific, non-universal, social content. It possesses only limited universality accorded by historically specific economic institutions. It is also limited because of restricted convertibility among currencies. To put it in another way, money is socially constructed as a universal medium within a limited domain of exchange. In its limited universality, however, modern money does establish a rule of equivalence among commodities, as qualitative differences between commodities become expressible in numbers, providing a medium for their exchangeability. For instance, $50 may congeal into a pair of shoes here or a set of DVDs there. Liquidity is nothing but the universality of acceptance with passive trust in the system.

Discussions of money as a universal medium abound. Talcott Parsons

(1977) analyzed money as a medium that steers intersystemic exchanges between goods and labor power. Habermas (1988) extends this analysis of money to argue that the institutionalization of money in bourgeois civil law, especially property and contract law, resulted in the conversion of previously noneconomic environments into money-steered economic subsystems. This monetization, according to Habermas, was as important as the rise of the capitalist enterprise for the new mode of production, when "production was converted to wage labor and the state apparatus was connected back to production through the taxes of the employed." The state itself became dependent on the monetarily steered economic subsystem. Money also helped to convert labor into a commodity. Habermas reinterprets Marx's notion of the dual character of labor under capitalism, according to which labor belongs both to the person's lifeworld as a concrete action and to the economic system as an abstract performance organized, bought, and sold according to capital imperatives. Money as a steering medium helps to institutionalize the wage-labor relation under capitalism, neutralizing the lifeworld context of labor by rendering it abstract.

Programming languages, I argue, act as another steering medium, a common medium of work, enabling a conversion of concrete skills into abstract logical skills. While money acts on labor externally by making it exchangeable at the marketplace like a commodity, programming languages render labor abstract from within, as they abolish some of the particularities of concrete labor by turning different kinds of labor into software lines. The ability to break down, digitize, and then repackage into a program the mathematical skills of an accountant, a civil engineer's mathematical and visual conception of a three-dimensional structure, an architect's drawing skills, and some managerial decision-making skills enhances the potential for rearranging elements of work in different configurations. With the capacity for universal coding, software can be developed as readily for white-collar jobs as for the control of heavy industrial machinery, thereby occasioning a common medium of electronic texts and graphics across different jobs and occupations. As an Indian engineer pointed out, the job of a hardware engineer now "is mostly a software job. They say you're a hardware engineer, but you're actually out there writing programs to build the chip. In the olden days, it used to be a proper hardware job, which means that you take a soldering iron and wires, and you would fix them yourself. Now you sit in the front of your computer and you have these little pieces of software, which help you lay down wires on your screen; you don't have a real wire in hand, and you put transistors here and wires there. Then you simulate it to see if it works."

The rise of programming languages as a work medium is doubly significant. In addition to being one of the largest and fastest-growing occupations in the United States (Bureau of Labor Statistics 2000), with enormous influence on all work practices in general (McConnell 1996), software writing is a space where other technologies are imagined and invented. The medium of software facilitates the imagination of new car designs within the framework of their aerodynamic viability; it enables a simulation of the flight trajectories of space shuttles; it helps pilots to fly planes in a simulator before they control actual, software-enabled airplanes. Without the medium of programming languages, it would be nearly impossible to read the "book of life" and its complex sets of gene sequences.

The new universal medium of software is inextricably connected to the growing convergence of work skills, in both senses of the term "convergence." First, previously differentiated concrete forms of labor converge in a single, integrated software. For instance, software systems integrate many clerical skills—such as typing, editing, and formatting—into applications used by higher-level professionals, thereby making specialized, separate secretarial positions less useful. Second, concrete skills converge in terms of the similarity of the logic used to perform work. As more and more areas of work are being brought into the realm of computers, the new skills required of the previously heterogeneous workforce include the ability to think in terms of computer logic and to master logical structures common to different kinds of software. Consequently, there is enormous boundary crossing in postindustrial work settings. For instance, an informant noted that a large number of Ph.D. students in physics were being hired by Wall Street firms, not for their knowledge of physics but because of their keen logical ability, which makes it relatively easy for them to learn Structured Query Language and develop financial database software. To give another illustration of this aspect of skill convergence, people working in areas as varied as hardware and software, electrical and mechanical engineering, process engineering, and simple programming, whose earlier jobs and training greatly differed from each other, are now writing software for different purposes. During the study of skill transformations under information technologies in the earlier phase of my research, an electrical engineer pointed how his job now involved only software engineering:

> Even ten years ago, most electrical engineers had very little to do with software. In fact, most electrical equipment had no software connected to it, but over the years, a lot of things have shifted to software . . . most things have become digital, and once things become digital, they can be controlled using a computer. So, slowly, everything is shifting to computers. A lot of electrical design is now being done on computers, because it can be done much faster. Yes, over the last ten to fifteen years, there has been a very big shift in electrical engineering. Now, every electrical engineer must know programming languages, which wasn't the case some years ago. . . . If I were to start [my career] again, I'd start more so in computer science, because right now, I've slowly drifted from hard-core electrical engineering to software. So, if I were to start again, I might as well start in software, than waste my time doing electrical machines and controls.

With the convergence of previously differentiated domains of work, information skills divide themselves—at a general level—into two broad groups of workers: software users and software writers. Most workers belonging to diverse occupations—especially in advanced capitalist societies—are either using software programs or writing them. This distinction is not a strict boundary, as a software user writing macros is also a software writer at a reduced level of complexity. Yet the distinction may be useful for a clearer grasp of the growing abstraction of labor and the convergence of skills in the medium afforded by programming languages.

The "convergence" of skills certainly does not imply an "identity" of skills. A secretary using a database program is not executing the same set of skills as someone using a statistical software package, who must have a certain understanding of statistical principles. Yet in addition to relieving the worker from the burden of countless calculations, statistics software also—to a degree—makes unnecessary the knowledge of mathematics that is the basis for the calculations, making the two cases comparable. Despite the distinctions among various workers, the convergence of skills across different occupations results from constituting work as a problem of coding, and of further coding within codes, a sort of symbolic sedimentation. This idea is well expressed in the phrase "closer to the machine," used by software engineers to distinguish those who deal with the foundational or deeper layers of machine code from those who use higher-level programs called "applications." The structuring of work as a general problem of coding represents what I call the linguistification of labor. Programming as a linguistic activity resembles certain features of money. In a sense, modern money is a sign system; it is neither a commodity nor a production factor; it does not have any intrinsic value apart from symbolizing amounts of value. As such it is quite like programming languages, which are symbolic sedimentations of labor and knowledge, but linguistic symbols are not themselves this knowledge. Just as money can be converted into different commodities, programming code may also emerge as an image here or music there.

Consider an image that appeared on a web site and was forwarded to me by one of my students at Stanford a couple of years ago. The image is a form of digital art rendered through code. Interestingly, it is also a computer program, DECSS, that decodes the encryption scheme (CSS) employed to restrict the usage of DVD films on different devices. If you run the code written in the picture with the picture itself as the input, the output is the program DECSS. Thus the code is at once an image and a software program. It is also, to be sure, legal and illegal at the same time: both a legal, copyrightable image and an illegal code. The Digital Millennium Copyright Act of 1998 (DMCA) makes it a crime to "circumvent a technological measure that effectively controls access to a work protected" under the act. The convertibility afforded by code is massive, as it liquefies what were previously solid boundaries. One major question in the copyright debate is whether code may be considered free speech protected under the Constitution. Code written by a programmer in a programming language such as C or Java is human-readable and communicable *text*.[2] If code were indeed free speech, then instead of DECSS being declared illegal, certain clauses of the DMCA would be declared unconstitutional. To my understanding, code seems simultaneously to be *speech* and *machine* communicable as text, while capable of producing a predictable output like a machine. No wonder that the development of code challenges many existing laws based on different assumptions about boundaries that define objects. Just as money's liquidity depends on its linguistic nature as a system of signs and numbers, the liquidity of code relates to integration through language.

Many previous discussions of computer technologies have focused on tools or the tool contexts of computing. Pelle Ehn (1988) and Malcolm McCullough (1996), for instance, both attempt to advance our understanding of computer-mediated work in terms of designing digital artifacts. While Ehn proposes the language of artifacts to develop novel approaches to computer work for emancipatory purposes, McCullough maintains that recent technological advances have regained some of the holism of earlier craftwork that was lost during the industrial age. In craft work, manual and conceptual skills—a certain coordination of hands, eyes, and mind—were harmoniously combined in direct manipulation of real objects. McCullough claims that software programs such as MacPaint and MacDraw in the 1980s were the first direct manipulation programs, requiring hand-eye coordination instead of just typing numbers on a keyboard. The rise of such tools as CAD/CAM systems along with a number of other software such as graphic and paint programs, McCullough argues, means that a new technology is born "with old roots." Although it is true that we cannot boast of the "direct manipulation" of material objects as we did in traditional craft, we have regained some of its aspects in what may be called "indirect manipulation." Instead of being directly manipulable, our tools—symbolically represented in software—can be conceptually and indirectly controlled. In a paint program, for instance, one can look around for a paint or brush, pick it up, hold it, and move it into relation with other objects. Software of this kind, McCullough suggests, should be understood as a *mechanism* in our endeavor to produce what he calls "digital artifacts." In this view, CAD and CAM as mechanisms seem to converge with traditional artisanry in that they create three-dimensional things in a tightened loop between design and fabrication. Just as in traditional craft, a good design is grounded in fabrication and vice versa; in the CAD/CAM system, design variations and fabrication process criteria drive one another. In this coupling, "input to physical fabrication operation is symbolic, and the output from geometric derivations is tangible . . . Thus, after two centuries of separation, the conception and the execution of everyday objects are once again in the same hands" (McCullough 1996, 178). Some scholars do not completely subscribe to this view. Because new design alternatives are countless, in many CAD applications the designer is increasingly required to merely select from a "menu" of "optimized" alternatives, a limitation which may throttle rather than expand creativity (Shaiken 1986).

While discussions of computing in terms of artifacts are interesting and important, we must also look at computing in terms of language and liquidity. Armed with programming languages, economic practices are experiencing a paradigm shift from a materialistic tool-making enterprise to symbolic and linguistic imagination, from technology-as-a-tool to technology-as-code. Programming languages have become the ever-present horizon of work, as the taken-for-granted background that is "always already" there when we work. Programmed texts are not dead sediments of code, however, for they can execute commands. They are action scripts; they are machines, capable of doing things, enacting and interacting. The programmed texts can be organizations (enterprise systems), machines (simulated models of cars or space shuttles), consumable commodities (music, video games, movies, or pictures), or even money (transnational flows of finance capital). Like money, programming languages are "radical levelers" that do away with many distinctions. The intertranslatability and blurring of boundaries triggered by programming languages contributes to the birth of a transnational economy of signs that increasingly informs and influences the economy of goods. It is only in this context that we can talk of virtual migration, which is above all a flow of signs, pieces of codes, and texts. Flows of this kind fail to recognize nation-state boundaries, enabling a transnational programmability of processes through "language."

Language

In what respect could programming languages—such as BASIC, FORTRAN, Pascal, PROLOG, C++, or Java—be called languages? The history of computer software and, to a degree, hardware designs can be traced to a search for an "ideal language"—a language that is precise, unambiguous, and clear in structure, on the model of symbolic logic, in contrast to ordinary language, which is nebulous, misleading, and at times contradictory. Symbolic logic was intended to achieve the systematic closure of all equivocation, ambiguity, metaphorical play, and undecidability inherent in ordinary language.

The goal was to reduce the operation of linguistic signifiers to single, unequivocal referents, and attain saturation in language with predictable accuracy. The seventeenth-century philosopher and mathematician Gottfried Wilhelm Leibniz was the first to propose—perhaps after the Cartesian vision of universal mathematics—a "universally characteristic language" (*lingua characteristica universalis*), "a true alphabet of human thought" (Davis 2000). Such a language was supposed to represent concepts notationally by showing the more fundamental concepts of which they were composed. Once converted into universally symbolic forms, such as graphs and diagrams, these concepts would be understood by all readers, irrespective of their native language. In the late nineteenth century Giuseppe Peano (1973) developed Interlingua, an uninflected form of Latin that represented a vigorous pursuit of the Leibnizian conception of universal language. The pursuit of a logical language also inspired Gottlob Frege, Bertrand Russell, and Alfred North Whitehead, triggering the development of the logical language LOGLAN and the computer language PROLOG.

Leibniz also proposed a "calculus of reason" (*calculus ratiocinator*), which would permit the exhaustive manipulation of symbols according to established rules. The calculus would help either to discover new truths or to test proposed conclusions to see if they could indeed be deduced from the premises. Reasoning could thus mimic the operation of large sums in the manner of algorithms, and thus be free from individual errors and failures of creativity. Reasoned derivations could be verified and performed by machines, which makes Leibniz the first to contemplate the possibility of something like a computer. Leibniz's idea for building machines to deduce valid references was taken up by Charles Babbage, William Stanley Jevons, and Charles Sanders Pierce and his student Alan Marquan in the nineteenth century, work that culminated in the immense success of modern computers in the second half of the twentieth century. Although Leibniz prefigured George Boole's remarkably similar work by two centuries, Boole is widely recognized for initiating symbolic logic. Boolean algebra—whether an independent work or not—helped to create a binary system of logic, which turned out to be crucial for information theory. It constituted the basis for the circuit and transistor designs used in electronic digital computers.

In the twentieth century the attempt to dispense with linguistic ambiguity was reflected in the early view of Wittgenstein (1922) about the role of language in providing a "picture of reality." Truth-value, under this view, consists in making logical propositions with a one-to-one correspondence to reality. The early Wittgenstein and the early Russell imagined an ideal language that would act as a criterion for determining the meaning, or meaninglessness, of statements about the world. While the project of developing an ideal and logical language did not succeed in its original sense, especially when Wittgenstein (1972) totally turned around in his analysis of language, the influence of symbolic logic retained its value. Whitehead and Russell (1925), in an attempt to prove that logic precedes mathematics, showed how all pure mathematics can be deduced from certain ideas and maxims of formal logic, by the help of the logic of relations, without any undefined ideas or unproved propositions.

Most of the rationally consistent approaches to information theory, following Shannon and Weaver (1963), employ the structural rigors of formal logic, replacing the looser syntaxes, grammars, and vocabularies of ordinary languages along with their symbolic, poetic, and surplus meanings. One of my students at Stanford, Aditya Berlia, challenged my overemphasis on the lack of surplus meanings in code. Most programming languages are created in the scripts and semantics of real languages. Thus they inherit, he argues, the ability from these real languages to produce poetic forms. He provides an example of a love letter in code:

```
#include <my_heart.h>
#include <your_heart.h>
int main( )
{
love_you = 1;
bool me_alive = true;;
for (int I=love_you; me_alive = true ; I++)
{
cout << "I love you!";
}
}
```

This code will keep saying "I love you" until "me_alive" becomes false. Any programmer will be able to read this as a message without even having to compile it in a compiler: I will love you more and more (since "I" is increasing) until I die. So there are functions that can change their behavior depending on what one wishes to perform, or through interaction with the user. With enough variables, a multi-tiered system as complex and enjoyable as poetry can be created. Aditya further contended that code reflects the expression and style of the author, almost like a unique signature, which can be interpreted on multiple levels. Consider the following simple example:

```
#include<iostream.h>
main( ) {
cout << "Hello World! An example of Addition" <<endl; a = a + 1; cout << "A:"
<< A"; }
```

The above code in C++ is legitimate but to a good programmer, Aditya argues, it is an eyesore. The following version of the same expression is not only better but also tells a great deal about the personality and style of the programmer:

```
#include <iostream.h>
int main( )
{
cout << "Hello World! An example of Addition" << endl;
a++;
cout << "A:" << A";
return 0;
}
```

I agree with Aditya's contention that many would consider the second set of code more elegant than the first. While code does have, almost like ordinary languages, the possibility of economic and thus elegant expression, I do not think that this demolishes the difference between ordinary and programming languages for a simple reason: there would be no necessity of creating programming languages if ordinary languages could translate into machine language with equal ease, or perform a sufficient closure of meaning. The ultimate salvation of code lies in its merger with the machine. Cybernetic theory and computer technologies demand rigorous but uncomplicated languages to permit translation into nonambiguous, special symbols that can be stored and used for mathematical manipulations. The closed system of formal language proves ideal for this need. Conclusions drawn using syllogisms according to logical rules can be tested in a consistent, scientific manner, as long as all parties communicating share the rational premises employed by the particular system. The assumption of basic theorems of information theory is that the message transmitted is well organized, consistent, and characterized by relatively low and determinable degrees of entropy and redundancy.

All computer languages, informed by the rigors of formal logic, may be seen as a result of a certain formalization and functionalization of language, whereby the ambiguity and complexity of ordinary language are reduced to rationalized structures, with a high predictability of procedure and outcome. Ordinary languages, on the other hand, are grounded in a metaphorical play of endless referencing without a possibility of formal closure. This does not mean that programming languages are free of metaphors, for all language, including mathematics, is metaphoric—that is, an object of knowledge is always constituted in terms of its relation to something else, or else it would remain inexpressible.

The question is thus how differently metaphors are constituted in "ideal" and ordinary language, or in saturated and unsaturated linguistic structures. By my earlier definition of saturation in chapter 5, the question is relatively easy to answer. While formal language creates an artificial ground for metaphors, a place on which all fugitive meanings are strictly chained, ordinary language does not ground metaphors in a single referential domain, allowing free play and a certain undecidability to emerge. Students of symbolic logic recognize this difference, when they find out how difficult it is to translate multidimensional ordinary language sentences into calculable formal sentences of symbolic logic, strictly tying metaphors to unambiguous meanings in single bonds. Although the ability to close interpretive and ambiguous spaces for metaphoric play is an asset in software writing, it can also lead to problems. One basic problem with the traditional conception of artificial intelligence (AI) has been its assumption that the English language possesses a necessary and fairly simple underlying structure, which could be captured through formally defined algorithms or data structures (Dreyfus 1992), an assumption that misses the important shift by Wittgenstein (1972) from his earlier position. The later Wittgenstein viewed language more like a device whose use changes according to the context in which it is employed. Any attempt to codify how it operates through a closed set of rules might lead us to absurd results, for instance a belief that there are necessary rules limiting the use of a vegetable knife to the act of cutting vegetables only, forgetting that the knife might as well be used for opening a cardboard box or loosening a screw. Ordinary language is a social institution that is governed not by an external set of rules or a priori theories but only by what people view as correct and incorrect in different contexts.

Despite these concerns, programming skills normally demand strict adherence to tight structures. For instance, a programmer who uses Structured Query Language is bound to stick to a formally closed style of writing, such as "Select salary from payroll where employee='Erica.'" In short, the linguistic rationalization through symbolic logic is achieved by mechanically closing the play of surplus meanings and the undecidability of propositions. This closure of play spaces in programming languages is what makes algocratic schemes of governance possible. Code-based programming schemes, like all systems of governance, tend to reduce the negotiability of processes. Let me start the discussion of governance through code and money with the question of nonnegotiability.

Governance

All programming schemes, once implemented, erode the negotiability of processes. To recall my example of San Francisco streets (chapter 5), one may in principle negotiate with a traffic cop but not with a traffic video camera, which will take pictures as programmed. All negotiation must take place before the cameras are installed. True, a certain leniency, even artificial intelligence, might itself be programmed into video camera software. But there would not be any active space of negotiability in every case. After all, there would be no process of being physically stopped by the camera that would allow the negotiation process to take place. Either one's transgression was within the limits of acceptability or it was not. Unless feelings and socialization biases were coded into programming schemes, it would not be possible to allow a celebrity, for instance, to go unpunished for a traffic violation.[3] For the camera to be "lenient," like a gentle male cop toward a female Hollywood actress, programming schemes would need to be designed by heterosexual male programmers free to embed into the program facial exemptions based on their favorite female actresses. Surely it is not my contention that human police are somehow better than cameras because of the possibility of negotiation; there are too many examples of abuse and authoritarianism to pass such a judgment. In some respects the notion that everyone is equal before the law may perhaps be accomplished more easily once social interaction is replaced by the invisible interaction with code. All individual cases of class, race, and gender bias can be done away with by making traffic governance nonnegotiable and automatic (unless the cameras are installed only in certain neighborhoods). But nonnegotiability does reflect a regular and abstract exercise of power in a virtually controlled social space. Again, the control exercised by a programming scheme might be resisted by someone who was able to hack into the code of video surveillance, but that would be as rare as the act of killing a cop.

Governance schemes with reduced negotiability are becoming part of everyday life. Four of my students at Stanford gave another simple but generalizable example in a collaborative paper:[4]

> In looking for a smaller and more ubiquitous physical manifestation of technology at Stanford, one has to look no further than the Stanford University ID card. Using this card is an everyday event and students may not be aware of the technologies associated with this 3 3/8″ by 2 1/8″ piece of plastic. The Stanford ID is a standard card with a magnetic stripe, a bar code, and a chip that can be used for many things on campus. The card is used at the dining halls, at campus stores, at the libraries, and for accessing buildings after hours. Swiping the card with the magnetic stripe, scanning the bar code, and holding the card up to a wireless chip reader are ways that the card can be read. For instance, the Packard building is locked after 5 pm every day and students working in the Electric Engineering labs may unlock the laboratory and the front entrance by holding the card up to a card reader. Students do not need to remove their SUIDs from their wallets or purses. The consequence of this campus-wide deployment of ID card readers is that more services are becoming more convenient, students may have their locations and behavior monitored, and students are dependent on ID cards for their most fundamental needs.

While this governance system affords both convenience and security, it also reduces the need for interaction with the receptionist or guard with whom students might be able to negotiate an entry even if they forgot to bring their ID cards. Once the governance is transferred over to devices coded with rules, their effects are continuous and universal, and their rules non-negotiable.

Does money introduce a similar form of nonnegotiability in other spheres? Monetization does in fact establish an analogous independence from language-based negotiation in social life. Consider an ordinary, everyday event: moving out of one's house. In the United States there are two ways to move: asking others to help you move or hiring a moving company to pack up and move. One may depend on one's friends or neighbors to help one move from one place to another. Doing so requires many things: one must have friends in the first place; they must be close enough that one can ask them a favor; and one must be ready to carry the obligation for possible reciprocity in the future. The other way to move is to hire a moving company to perform the same task. In the second case, the monetization of service frees a person from negotiations with friends. A gradual monetization of all spheres of life, including child care and care for the aged, reduces the need for reaching everyday understanding with family members, neighbors, and social others, leaving social interactions with a slim linguistic veneer. The question is not only about instances of interaction but the cohesion of larger social life through webs of meaningful connections gained through personal commitments. Traditionally, social commitments and responsibility have been ways of finding meaning in life.[5] True, interactions in nursing homes are social as well, but these are professional commitments, derived primarily from instrumental relations of market exchange, and thus are different from noneconomic commitments and obligations.

In social theory, the transfer of noneconomic, everyday commitments to the economic realm is a well-acknowledged example about money as a steering medium of action: "Media such as money and power encode a purposive-rational attitude toward calculable amounts of value and make it possible to exert generalized, strategic influence on the decisions of other participants while *bypassing* processes of consensus-oriented communication. Inasmuch as they do not merely simplify linguistic communication but *replace* it with a symbolic generalization of rewards and punishments, the lifeworld contexts in which processes of reaching understanding are always embedded are devalued in favor of media-steered interactions; the lifeworld is no longer needed for the coordination of action" (Habermas 1988, 183). When social interaction is increasingly steered through the symbolic medium of money, it also goes beyond local contexts, for money, like code, is a technique of communication, linking up interactions across space and time. "The power of money to bridge distances," Simmel notes, "enables the owner and his possessions to exist so far apart that each of them may follow their own precepts to a greater extent than in the period when the owner and his possession still stood in direct mutual relationship, when every economic engagement was also a personal one" (Simmel 1990, 333). As money affords exchanges at a distance, it connects activities, like code, across space and time, producing the possibility of global integrations.

The relationship of money and space has been lucidly explored by Leyshon and Thrift (1997) in *Money/Space*, in which they detail the historical characteristics of money in terms of the conquest of space and time for economic purposes. Evidently, the effort to convert commodities into monetary symbols and the communication of those symbols across space and time were related projects. The integration of space and time through code, as I discussed in chapter 5, is not far from the integration produced through monetary techniques. In fact, one can link the dominance of the coin as a monetary form to the governmental expansion of the Roman Empire and its propagation of commodity money.

Commodity money was connected with territorial integration and imperial governance in Europe. Between 600 BC and AD 400, during the Roman Empire, coinage worked as the basis of Europe's monetary systems (Davies 1994). With the collapse of the Roman Empire, commodity money as the dominant monetary form also disappeared from parts of Europe for hundreds of years (Spufford 1988). The revival of the commodity money form once again coincided with the ascendance of the European monarchical state. A consistent, standardized system of coinage was a way to ensure the worth of tributes and taxation extracted by the state from its subjects, and the extent of its spread also signaled the extent of the state's territorial boundaries. "Coins followed—indeed accompanied—the sword," for the development of coinage facilitated military action at a distance and pay for the troops and camp followers (Davies 1994, 108). "As the armies went on their military campaigns they became vehicles of monetary expansion and incursion, for they took their coins with them, which subsequently became used as money in the territories they appropriated. The effect of these actions was to bring about a degree of financial integration over space. One way in which this came about, of course, was through direct force, as more powerful states imposed their money on weak states, thereby easing economic integration and eliminating uncertainties associated with monetary exchange" (Leyshon and Thrift 1997, 24). Clearly the history of the standardized commodity money form is linked with programs of integration, therefore governance, across expansive territories. But the commodity money still needed enormous effort to haul it over long distances. "Eventually and inexorably paper was to displace silver and gold, and thereby to release money from its metallic chains and anchors" (Davies 1994, 174).

Compared to commodity money, what is termed the *money of account* (Leyshon and Thrift 1997) emerges as a subtler technique of communication and governmental integration. For international trade to grow, it was important to overcome the problem of the multiplicity of commodity currencies. There developed a new technique and a new form of money, the bill of exchange, which also solved the problem of the physical transport of coin and ingot across difficult and dangerous territorial space. The bill of exchange was a new technique of communication by which the need to barter or make payments in coin or ingot could be avoided. This form of money was thus a technique of distantiation. Face-to-face interactions for clearing books were no longer necessary. Money of account thus comes very close to my discussion in chapter 5 of spatial integrations through code.

While it is easy to understand how money effected spatial integration, one may ask how the question of time figures in this discussion. The temporal factor in money arises because of the institutional promise that money can be made good in the future. A simple historical example should serve the purpose. As early as the twelfth century, the exchequer of receipt in England was issuing "tallies," an ancient form of providing evidence of payment, so that the king's creditor could directly collect payment from the king's original debtor. But the circulation of tallies became a problem for those who had to traverse the entire length of the territory to find the counterparty to the tally they were holding. This impediment led to the development of a new monetary technique whereby merchants would enable the tally holders to take a temporal leap by letting them take immediate delivery of commodity money at a discounted price, saving them the time and expense involved in finding the counterparty. Money of account appears as a temporal short cut, or rather a continuous deferment of payment across space and time. The liquidity of even hard cash, the ease with which it can be converted into goods, is based on passive trust, as one takes its future convertibility for granted, even though economic downturns can wipe out trillions of dollars on a single day (as they did on 19 October 1987).

Code increases the liquidity of money across space and time. As code enables an almost immediate authorization of loans through the use of credit cards, credit worthiness itself has been turned into money. Money may be understood as a special kind of code by means of which information travels from a sender to a receiver in a symbolic form (Parsons 1977). Plastic money—a hybrid form in which money flows as code within the channels provided by another layer of code—may not be included in M1, money's most liquid form, but with the increasing universality of acceptance it is attaining a liquidity that had earlier been reserved only for hard cash. But plastic money is a little more than money. It bundles aspects of control in its very functioning, such as by providing an automatic identity check, required for car rentals or hotel reservations. If one breaks the car or steals something from the hotel room, the credit card allows the damage to be charged post facto as an incidental.

As with the monetary interweaving of the world economy, code also makes it possible for labor to flow and intermingle at a global level. Thus virtual migration is made possible by an important development in the nature of labor itself, which is the liquefaction of concrete labor into signs and symbols, into a form of communication, into code. Programming languages have emerged as currencies, facilitating—like money—a diversity of flows into images, sounds, and texts. What has enabled labor thereby to increasingly become "information labor" or communication is programming. Therefore there is an important shift in the nature of labor itself, which I have elsewhere called the linguistic turn of technology (Aneesh 2001). The reason why programming and associated forms of labor can move in cyberspace relates in an important sense to this transformation. By converting a range of tasks into a problem of coding, programming languages enable constant online access and monitoring across continents, environment cloning, and online shipping of work, and thus make possible a transnational labor regime that increasingly competes with the still strong international order of shipping the bodies, as in body shopping, across national boundaries.

CHAPTER 7

Migrations:
Nation, Capital, and the State

One of the great social crises of this country is unrestricted immigration and an invasion from the south. — Pat Buchanan (2000)

Aggregated demand is putting very significant pressures on an ever-decreasing available supply of unemployed labor. The one obvious means that one can use to offset that is expanding the number of people we allow in . . . So, I think reviewing our immigration laws in the context of the type of economy, which we will be enjoying in the decade ahead, is clearly on the table in my judgment. — Alan Greenspan, Chairman, Federal Reserve Board, *Testimony before the U.S. House of Representatives Committee on Banking and Financial Services, July 22, 1999*

Mr. Chairman, I commend you and the other members of your Committee for your efforts in . . . establishing immigration policies that give our industry and other high-tech companies access to the best and the brightest resources. — Bill Gates, *Statement before the Committee on the Judiciary, United States Senate, March 3, 1998*

The three statements above about immigration into the United States are grounded in three separate discursive spaces: nation, state, and capital. Accordingly, the first quote is a nationalistic, patriotic battle cry that likens immigration to an invasion; in the second quote, immigration is a source of labor, driven by the calm and calculated rationality of the economic system; and in the third quote, immigration is a resource to be harnessed for production and profit. Nationalist discourse, based on a logic of total closure, is almost always opposed to immigration in general, imagining the nation as a closed body that must defend its organic purity against foreign elements.

Capitalist discourse, on the other hand, almost always encourages immigration, for it ensures an adequate reserve of skilled and unskilled labor while keeping wages at a profitable level. The state is caught between these two opposing demands of nation and capital, in addition to the systemic pressures of providing economic growth for its own legitimacy in a democracy.[1] Labor immigration is a source of tension between these different programs of control and governance.

Discourses of nation and transnational capital share a particularly uneasy relationship with respect to the status and flow of workers. Nationalist discourses have depended on territorial integrity and historical or cultural identity, distinguishing clearly between citizens and foreigners. Discourses of capital are independent—at least in principle—of such distinctions at the level of abstract labor power as well as at the level of the laboring body, which emerges as a bundle of skills without the necessity of national identity marks.[2] This troubled relationship expresses itself in the constant tug of war played out in the U.S. Congress between nationalist and corporate lobbies. Nationalist pressures tend to force Congress to collect migration data, to intensify border policing, impose restrictions on immigration, and control the activities of American corporations abroad. Capital twists the state's arms in the other direction, forcing the state to relax immigration quotas. For instance, when the Republican Senator Alan Simpson introduced a bill in 1995 to impose deep cuts on legal immigration levels in accordance with the nationalist agenda, Bill Gates called the bill an "absolute disaster." "If you want to prevent companies like ours from doing work in the United States," he warned, "this is a masterpiece" (Mills 1995). Simpson withdrew many provisions in his bill and said, "All the things that Bill Gates was concerned about are no longer there. After two weeks of watching the reaction of the business community . . . I knew pretty well where we were headed" (Cao 1995). In response to such conflicting pressures, the state has long followed a revolving door policy (Cockcroft 1986), easing immigration flows when the economy is on the upswing and the business demand for labor is high, and restricting and even deporting immigrants during economic downturns when nationalist resentment against immigrants tends to rise.

It is not surprising that the Bureau of Citizenship and Immigration Services (BCIS, formerly the Immigration and Naturalization Service), the executive arm of the state in charge of regulating immigration, has long been caught between the opposite pulls of transnational capitalism, which demands a free flow of both capital and labor, and the nationalist reaction against an increasing "alien invasion" of its sacrosanct boundaries. In the last few decades border enforcement has immensely expanded, with increased funds for both old technologies dating to the Vietnam years and the latest computer and tracking technologies. A strategy called "concentrated border enforcement" provides for ten-foot-high fences made from surplus corrugated steel landing mats along the southwest border, remote video surveillance linked to in-ground sensors, portable and stationary high-intensity lighting, thousands of border patrol agents, mobile infrared night scopes that use thermal imaging to detect migrants by their body heat, motion detecting sensors buried in the ground near the border, airborne infrared radars, and a computerized system of biometric scanning called IDENT, which records photographs, fingerprints, and biographical data along with the date and location of a migrant's apprehension (Cornelius 2001). Borrowed from the Defense Department and applied to immigration control at the border, military technologies that were originally designed for Vietnam and Central America have turned the border into a militarized zone (Dunn 1996). New modes of interagency collaboration have broadened and extended federal police powers regarding deportation decisions and other matters to state and local authorities.

As the discourse of nation tends to revolve around a certain conception of the body as bearing national identity marks, the obstinate concern with the immigrant's body in the United States becomes understandable. The policy of free and open immigration continued in the United States until a large number of groups such as Irish, German, and Chinese immigrants began arriving toward the end of the mid-nineteenth century. While the passing of the Chinese Exclusion Act in 1882 may have been the most visible act of exclusion, the entire setup of immigrant inspection ports centered on whether the immigrant possessed a physically and mentally healthy body. As early as 1892, new arrivals at Ellis Island were inspected in detail. Until 1909 the national enterprise of inspecting immigrants for their fitness to join the new nation was initially financed by an "immigrant fund" established with collections from a head tax on immigrants paid by ship companies or ship captains. Unhealthy and diseased immigrants, including "lunatics" and "idiots," were detained at the port and deported at the expense of the transportation company that had brought them to the United States. The concern with the immigrant body was not necessarily always negative. The Dillingham Immigration Commission, for instance, employed such a respected anthropologist as Franz Boas to see if later generations of immigrants physically and mentally benefited from their stay in the United States. The carefully conducted study by Boas measured and compared the rate of physiological development of the foreign-born and the American-born, focusing on probable causes of change in type. "In most of the European types that have been investigated," the report (Dillingham 1911, 5) concluded, "the head form, which has always been considered one of the most stable and permanent characteristics of human races, undergoes far-reaching changes coincident with the transfer of the people from European to American soil. For instance, the east European Hebrew, who has a very round head, becomes more long-headed; the south Italian, who in Italy has an exceedingly long head, becomes more short-headed; so that in this country both approach a uniform type, as far as the roundness of the head is concerned." While the argument was surely against racial stability, and thus racism, one cannot overlook the nationalistic concern with the body in the study.

In India the emigration of skilled labor has long been a source of heated debate, and consequences of the "brain drain" have been a matter of nationalist concern. The nationalist discourse has also constantly resisted the feared hegemony of multinational corporations since independence. These nationalist pressures are reflected in many state actions, such as the expulsion of Coca-Cola in 1977 and the attempted cancellation of contracts with the Enron Corporation in 1996 by a nationalist party that came to power in the state of Maharashtra.[3] Transnational companies tend to stir memories of colonization, which was initiated not by Britain but by a British trading company in the eighteenth century. The governmental integration rooted in the transnational colonialism of the nineteenth century had simultaneously given rise to a modern national space and a nationalist consciousness opposed to colonialism.

The discourse of capital, on the other hand, asserts that for markets to be "free," labor should be allowed to move as freely as goods do under free trade, in accordance with demand and supply principles. Corporations in the United States have long cherished the idea of an unhindered inflow of foreign labor as well as fewer restrictions on their moving overseas. Corporate lobbying in Congress was responsible for massive increases in H1-B visa limits in the late 1990s, as mentioned in chapter 2. The unity of the capitalist discourse expresses itself in similar lobbying efforts carried out in the United States by the Indian software industry. In 1999 a spokesperson for Nasscom in Delhi freely acknowledged the lobbying efforts that the organization carried out in the United States to promote its transnational interests: "We have been working rather actively . . . in the U.S. In fact, the recent H1-B amendment that you hear about in which they announced an increase of 50,000 for the new quota for the H1-B visas, starting on October 1 and lasting through September 30th 1999, we feel we acted as a major catalyst in driving that . . . Even much before that [we have been] lobbying with the Capitol Hill on various issues like Social Security to taxes and so on and so forth. Because we feel various kinds of taxes and . . . demands that are put forth by the revenue service department of U.S. government are basically tantamount to double taxation on allowances given to the software engineers working in the USA."[4]

The tension between corporate lobbying and nationalist resistance is played out in the patio of the state, which increasingly balances the two pressures. As discussed in chapter 2, different agencies of the state (the Department of Labor, the Department of State, and the Department of Justice), while governing the same populace, may assume different postures as they are collectively required to both control and facilitate labor immigration. Many legislative acts similarly display Congress's attempt to juggle various pressures. For example, while the American Competitiveness in the Twenty-First Century Act of 2000 increased the number of H-1B visas to 195,000 a year for the next three years, a result of corporate lobbying, the act also demands, under nationalist pressures, that employers pay a $1,000 fee for each H-1B application, with the funds used to generate $150 million a year for scholarships for U.S. nationals.

With the rise of virtual migration, however, the state and capital may have negotiated a truce in the electronic space of online labor flows. Practices of virtual migration at once allow the unhampered movement of labor and skills and prevent alien cultural bodies from crossing national spaces. The software firms are able to provide real labor at a global level; yet both workers in India and corporations in the United States remain on their local national turf. Virtual mobility allows the state to substantially dilute its control over labor flows while keeping and even reinforcing its territorial control by limiting the flow of laboring bodies across national borders. Thus the transnational forces of algocratic integration both surpass and succumb to state-based territoriality. With newly gained flexibility in labor supply through transnational virtual migration, contemporary capitalism also seems to have found solutions to two major problems. First, corporations can avoid confrontation with nationalist politics on the issue of alien immigration, because they can harness foreign labor online without a visa, bypassing the always opposed politics of national culture and identity. In contrast to physical migration, which brings in humans along with the labor — demanding tolerance for cultural difference, education for their children, a possible long-term settlement, and general social security from the affluent society — virtual labor flows do not require that alien humans join the nation. Second, the invisibility of virtual labor helps American corporations avoid the charge that they would rather hire immigrants than citizens.

Where are the state and its supposed sovereignty amid such developments? Perhaps it is inadequate, as I contended earlier, to see the state as a sovereign unit, as implied in various discourses of the state. The state probably never had this sovereignty, unity, or rigorous functionality; it was perhaps no more than a composite reality and a mythicized abstraction with limited importance (Foucault 1991). What is important is the administrative rationality that informs various activities on both sides of the constructed public and private divide. The transnational apparatus that makes virtual labor migration possible extends from political institutions to private corporations, from corporate satellites to state satellites, from fiberoptic cables running under transnational waters and national territories to ubiquitous computer screens, from privately owned telecommunications to publicly owned telecom sectors.

Virtual labor migration is an important element of various programs of globalization pursued by state and corporate agencies. States have agreed — as reflected in the WTO's Declaration on Global Electronic Commerce — to keep electronic services free from regulatory obstacles such as customs duties and tariffs. In fact the United States, in a submission to the WTO, suggested creating a permanent duty-free environment: "The most unambiguous way to ensure liberalized customs treatment of electronic commerce is to make permanent the moratorium on customs duties on electronic transmissions" (World Trade Organization 1999). National governments would thus benefit most by being less national, because "the rate at which electronic commerce brings benefits to any particular country will depend on how fast it liberalizes its market . . . The open global economy places a premium on characteristics inherent to electronic commerce—the ability to respond to markets without concern for geography and time through a medium that is ubiquitous and instantaneous" (World Trade Organization 1999). Couched under the broad term "electronic commerce," the increasingly free-flowing labor consists of telemarketing, customer service, the processing of insurance claims, medical transcription, data digitization, back-office operations, and accounting, in addition to programming. Although the flow of labor in a sense is "commerce," that is, a commercial exchange of labor in an increasingly transnational labor market, the choice not to call it labor migration or labor flow has something to do with the dominance of national states and their territorial enclosures, since transnational governmental integration itself is achieved through state-based governmental mechanisms.

Some state agencies in India, as partners in corporate programs of globalization, actively promote the transnational interests of the software industry. Recently a ministry of information technology was created in 1999 to convert "red tape into a red carpet" in the interest of the software industry (Nasscom 2000). There is nothing new about the government's promotion of business and industry. Peter Evans (1995) has explained at length the state's developmental role in terms not of the degree of involvement in industrial transformation but its kind. He distinguishes between two ideal types: predatory states such as Mobutu's Zaire that "extract at the expense of society, undercutting development even in the narrower sense of capital accumulation," and developmental states such as South Korea that have not only "presided over industrial transformation but can be plausibly argued to have played a role in making it happen" (12). Evans noticed a kind of shift in India's Department of Electronics in the mid-1980s from what he calls a custodial role to midwifery or husbandry, that is, from a regulatory and licensing role to a more promotional stance. In the 1990s corporate pressures for better infrastructure such as uninterrupted power supplies and fast telecommunication lines, coupled with the removal of some regulatory obstacles, have made for greater administrative integration within and between national spaces, and also signaled a clear shift in the state's developmental role in the information technology industry.

What is of importance for our discussion here is the transnational character of India's developmental efforts. Global administrative integration requires certain changes in existing state structures, such as the creation of transnational spaces within national territories. In the last few years the government of India has created many "greenhouses" such as Export Processing Zones (EPZs). Separated from the domestic tariff area, these are transnational enclaves where export production is organized on an internationally competitive basis with requisite infrastructure and duty-free imports (Nasscom 2000). These zones—currently in Kandla, Santa Cruz (Mumbai, Maharashtra), Cochin (Kerala), Chennai (Tamil Nadu), Vishakhapatanam (Andhra Pradesh), Falta (West Bengal), and Noida (Uttar Pradesh)—are exempt from basic, additional, and countervailing customs duties, with no requirement of licenses for imports. They are also exempt from the Central Excise Duty and other levies on all production that occurs there. Being transnational enclaves, there is no restriction on foreign shareholders in companies that set up units in EPZs. To cap it all, a ten-year tax holiday is available to the units based in EPZs,[5] in addition to exemption from income tax on profits derived from the export of software or software-enabled services. Although the government of India has failed to provide decent infrastructure at the national level, it has established Software Technology Parks (STPs) that enjoy, in addition to the tax holiday, an exemption from duty on all capital goods imports and better infrastructural resources, including high-speed data-communication facilities, a more dependable power supply, buildings, and other amenities. STP units, currently in Pune, Bangalore, Hyderabad, Bhubaneshwar, Chennai, Thiruvanathapuram, Gandhinagar, Noida, Kanpur, Indore, Panaji, Jaipur, and Calcutta, may be set up anywhere in India.

These transnational spaces—with direct connections to corporate sites around the world—are thus allowed to bypass the national space both in terms of taxation and the domestic market with which they have no inter-course. This case instantiates the questioning by Saskia Sassen (1997) of two prevalent propositions that rely on the duality of the global and the national: first, what the global economy gains the national state loses, and vice versa; and second, if an event such as a business transaction takes place in a na-tional territory, it is necessarily a national event. The global economy is not a phenomenon divorced from national states, and the national event is not merely "national." For a better understanding, we need a certain concep-tion of transnational administrative integration, which suggests asymmetric as well as site-specific integration. It is asymmetric because labor travels, like its physical counterpart, from low- to higher-wage markets. It is also site-specific because practices of integration do not involve all places on the globe equally, leaving vast regions such as southern Africa mostly untouched by infrastructural investments in training and technologies of integration. Un-like transport-based, spatially congruous globalization, this is a nodal form of globalization in which electronic commerce, algocratically integrated, hops from node to node with scant regard for places in between. The new form of globalization differs from the earlier period of capital expansion mostly in terms of the mode of integration, the basic character of which is algocratic. We must engage with the substantive flows of capital and commodities as well as with algocratic modes of integration that make such flows possible in the first place. The programmability and intertranslatability of processes across continents require us to rethink the categories with which we try to make sense of organizational change and governance and assess their effects on laboring populations.

The global economy is not purely global and national states are never completely national in another sense as well. Amid heated debates on job outsourcing to India, John Edwards (2004), promoting his candidacy for the Democratic presidential nomination in 2004, said, "The real solution is to outsource this [Bush] administration." This one-liner kept reverberating in Democratic politics throughout the election year, resurfacing here and there in John Kerry's campaign. Perhaps Edwards could not grasp the meaning of his own statement. Outsourcing does not mean mere expelling but rather getting the job done elsewhere. The unintended suggestion in his statement was that the American administration should be run not by someone like

Edwards but by someone in a place like India who could do it cheaply and efficiently. But on closer inspection his statement did inadvertently signify an interesting phenomenon: the national can take place outside the bounds of nation. For instance, federal and state taxes are the backbone of any administration. There is a whole national discourse organized around taxes in the United States. Yet some of this presumably national endeavor was indeed taking place in India during Edwards's campaign: about 150,000 federal and state tax returns were being prepared in India. With time-zone differences, workers in India could prepare tax returns while their clients slept. A taxpayer could drop off her financial documents at her accountant's office in the afternoon and have her tax return completed by morning. Major American accounting firms, such as Ernst & Young, obtained tax statistics from clients and allowed the workers in India to log on to secure servers based in the United States, retrieving and entering relevant information with tax-preparation software and sending the completed tax return to be filed in the United States. The national can indeed be decomposed into identifiable scripts that may move online across otherwise militarized borders. Yet the nationalist discourse is so strong that in most cases firms did not disclose that their tax returns were prepared overseas.

The virtual mobility of labor bears some resemblance to the mobility of capital. George Soros (1998), an international investor, maintains that financial markets are intrinsically unstable, a situation made worse by the lack of effective international mechanisms against destabilizing capital flows. The Asian financial crisis of the late 1990s exposed acute vulnerabilities of economies to the volatility of capital. In a world of hypermobile capital, a slight drop in confidence among international investors can result in a flight of capital that can leave national economies and their national sovereignty in the rubble. Although the virtual mobility of labor is not nearly as great as capital mobility, the integration enabled by code has similar actual and possible destabilizing effects on social life. The temporization of work is already with us and job displacements are on the rise. Protests like those staged in Seattle will perhaps be part of our foreseeable future.

I intended the comparison between code and money in chapter 6 as a way to illustrate the analytically distinguishable modes of global integration. Code is not capital. Because capital is always behind code, one may forget that code has distinctive capabilities of creating new forms of globalization. By algocratically connecting labor in different continents, the programming of globalization makes people dependent on, and at the mercy of, a transnational system that increasingly disregards state-based controls as well as protections afforded by labor unions while nation-states themselves partake in transnational governance structures. Thus it is no longer enough for labor unions in the United States to oppose high-tech immigration, because the quiet flow of virtual labor is becoming nearly as effective as actual physical labor migration. The growing interdependence of labor markets surely signals greater vulnerabilities. The question is not limited to how a decline in demand for labor in the United States directly influences the employment situation in India, or to how the relative ease with which work can be shifted outside the United States through data servers that are universally accessible to workers in India increases the possibility of job displacements and layoffs, even if temporary, in the United States. The question also pertains to larger issues of integrating temporally isolated pockets of social life in a way that has far-reaching significance in terms of the ever-growing subordination of the social to the economic. Solutions within the nation-state model may not suffice for problems that have transnational origins. As practices of programming bring together and integrate many other forms of labor around the world, they not only integrate social life in real time; they also disintegrate it by alienating it from its own surroundings. The phenomenon, historically unprecedented, questions the very foundations of social solidarity around the world.

A Note on Method

There were three objectives that informed this study of virtual migration: *critical, comparative,* and *exploratory,* each oriented toward a set of questions. The *critical objective* was to clarify the new "forms" of labor practice, i.e., how online programming worked. Rather than limit the inquiry to the questions of "what" was achieved and accomplished through new labor practices, what the content of work was, or what competitive advantages corporations gained by subcontracting online labor, I began by asking the question: "How" did one work? This question brought out the contours of a new regime of labor practice, which required new analytical tools to understand transformations in labor migration and how work is organized. As I pointed out earlier, online practice is too easily inserted into old schemata and codes of understanding. It is either ascribed to the trade schema of "export-import" or to the organizational schema of "subcontracting" and "outsourcing." The self-understanding of international and organizational economics treats the new regime as a mere extension of previous structures. I have attempted to question the certitude of self-evident continuity and linearity of economic understanding by making noneconomic aspects of the practice visible. I have also tried to show how the programming of globalization is possible through the marriage of two relatively independent historical trajectories of code and capital. Economic globalization is surely economic and capitalistic. But it is also noneconomic in its social effects as well as in its constitution, deriving from a particular history of philosophical symbolic logic. It is only through this understanding that I could make sense of a multiplicity of processes, including organizational, or algocratic, aspects of virtual migration.

From a *comparative perspective,* I inquired how different the virtual migration of information labor was from the physical migration of labor from India to the United States, especially in its social dimensions. I sought to identify how different mechanisms of global integration had different social effects on the physically migrating group and the group that stayed in India. I tried to examine the social, economic, and political implications for programmers working online from India as compared to migrant programmers working in the United States. Second, although body shopping is still widespread, virtual migration was found to be growing at a faster rate than its physical counterpart, a tendency that was partly corroborated by Nasscom's assertion that because of "unnatural visa restrictions," the offshore component of programming labor was on the rise. I also sought to compare the two practices not merely as economic activities, but more concretely as social practices.

The *exploratory objective* related to the study and exploration of a relatively understudied phenomenon. As mentioned earlier, information technologies, because of their peculiar effects, allow more and more areas of work to be turned into a problem of universal coding, converting into screen interaction different kinds of work that were earlier performed in a variety of ways. A related question that inspired this project was what forms of power could be embedded in software architectures themselves. The search for an answer led this research to articulate algocratic forms of governance as analytically distinct from other modes of governance.

Field Research

Procedurally, field research consisted of a multi-method approach to data collection, with nonparticipant observation and ethnographic interviews complementing a study of legislations on migration, labor, and information technologies as well as annual reports of the National Association of Software and Service Companies and technology magazines published in India. About half of more than a hundred interviews were formally tape-recorded; these interviews were with programmers, systems analysts, project managers, call center workers, human resource managers, and high-level executives, including CEOs, managing directors, and vice-presidents. Interviews were mainly conducted in the two languages in which I have requisite proficiency: Hindi and English.

Because two groups of workers composed the population of research interest—online labor and body-shopping labor—research was of necessity conducted in India as well as the United States in three phases. To sort out the workings of the two practices, I carried out field research from January 1999 to June 2000. As virtual migration was the main focus of this research, the first and last segments of fieldwork were conducted in India for six months each. In the first phase of research, from January to June 1999, programmers and project managers in New Delhi, Noida, and Gurgaon—a northern hub of software firms in India—were interviewed. During the second phase, from July to December 1999, programmers as well as high-level business executives were interviewed in New Jersey and surrounding areas. One of the important reasons for selecting New Jersey as a site of study was the prevalence of large and small high-tech corporations that employed many Indian programmers. Most of the programmers interviewed in the United States immigrated as a result of body shopping. In the last phase of research, in India from January to June 2000, mostly high-level executives—CEOs, managing directors, and vice-presidents of small, mid-size, and large software firms, again based in New Delhi, Gurgaon, and Noida—were interviewed.

In addition to interviews, field research consisted of multiple visits to twenty small, mid-size, and large software firms in New Delhi, Gurgaon, and Noida. The selection of software firms was facilitated by a directory published by the National Association of Software and Service Companies for the region. These software firms provided not only programming labor to the firms in the United States but also, as mentioned earlier, other forms of labor—telemarketing, accounting, technical support, design, and animation—based on software applications running on globally accessible data servers. Although the examples used in the book are relatively self-evident to the practitioners of online labor, in their micro details they inform larger debates on globalization, transcending the specific site of inquiry.

Given the lack of sociological research on globally operating software firms, field research afforded the empirical basis for analyzing screen-mediated social actions on the shop floor. It also revealed the importance of the algorithm, of programming and software applications, for even those forms of work, such as work carried out by call centers, that seem to lack an immediate relation to software development. My presence in the field generated richer material and permitted a more nuanced analysis than would have been possible by using standardized interview tools. Without actually observing the work processes, it would not have been possible to understand the integrative mechanisms of transnational software platforms that allow two teams based in different locations to work on the same project.

Of the twenty firms selected for study, designated "C1" to "C20," seven were foreign subsidiaries while thirteen were Indian-owned (see Appendix B). Foreign investment in software has been important since the beginning of the information technology industry in India a few decades ago. The firms ranged in size from over eleven thousand employees (C4) to fewer than ten (C11), quite representative of a young industry which has at present escaped excessive consolidation. The largest firm, C4, represents top-tier customized software development among the world's largest software firms and has continuously been ranked as one of the five or ten most profitable software firms worldwide. In keeping with the exponential growth of software industry in India, the size and revenue of these firms has roughly doubled since this research was conducted. Big and mid-size firms (three hundred employees and above) tend to have many branches both inside and outside India that help them synchronize their operations worldwide. While the majority of the clients of these firms were located in the United States, many of the firms also served clients in Europe, Japan, and the Middle East.

The analysis of ethnographic notes and interviews was facilitated by QSR's N5 software program, a handy tool for consolidating the data in terms of recurring themes under specified logical structures. This software accepted different kinds of data such as interviews, images, and legislative texts, and helped continuously fine-tune the analytical categories and introduce rigor into their interrelationships.

The question of method is however larger than mere procedures. The value of this book does not lie in the presentation of data. Instead of producing a data-driven study informed by what Portes (1997) calls "individual self-reports," I attempted the critical ethnography not of people or corporations but of a practice. The most important task was not to produce an "opinion poll" caught up within existing schemata, but to situate the practice within larger transformations. I attempted an ascending analysis of virtual migration, starting not from the lofty heights of global capitalism but from micro mechanisms of code, organization, and power. It is only when I looked at concrete techniques of code and communication that I was able to see how emerging practices were invested, transformed, and extended by general forms of transnational capitalism.

Thus I hope readers will read the book not for its presentation of facts, however rigorous and verifiable they may be, but for the new connections made and self-evident categories breached. Methodologically, this was not an attempt to produce yet another study of subcontracting and outsourcing. Instead, the aim was to break free from existing perspectives that dominate our understanding of online transnational labor practices, and to employ a different analytical perspective that illuminates even the most familiar, mundane aspects of the practice in fresh and surprising ways. It was important not to merely reproduce the views of programmers or executives but also to show how their statements were already part of a corporate discourse deeply invested in different forms of integration. While analyzing the everyday discourse and practices in the world of programming, I tried to make visible the emerging connections among organizational governance, labor migration, and their social costs and effects. Another contribution that I wished to make was to produce fresh concepts and analytical tools (virtual migration, total closure, skill saturation, algocracy) with which to think about recent global transformations, attempting to break free from the tendency to encase the transformation in older categories, or capture the different through the familiar. In short, I have tried to construct a fresh experience of global changes for the reader, who will be the ultimate judge of whether the effort has been successful.

Tables

TABLE I

*Companies with Largest Number of H-1B Petitions
Approved by the INS, October 1999 to February 2000*

1. Motorola	618
2. Oracle	455
3. Cisco Systems	398
4. Mastech	389
5. Intel	367
6. Microsoft	362
7. Rapidigm	357
8. Syntel	337
9. Wipro	327
10. Tata Consultancy Service	320
11. PriceWaterhouseCoopers	272
12. People Com Consultants	261
13. Lucent Technologies	255
14. Infosys Technologies	239
15. Nortel Networks	234
16. Tekedge	219
17. Data Conversion	195
18. Tata Infotech	185
19. Cotelligent USA	183
20. Sun Microsystems	182
21. Compuware	179
22. KPMG	177
23. Intelligroup	161
24. Hi Tech Consultants	157
25. Group Ipex	151

Source: U.S. Immigration and Naturalization Service, *Leading Employers of Specialty Occupation Workers (H-1B): October 1999 to February 2000* (2000).

TABLE 2

Country of Birth of Specialty Occupation Workers (H1-B)

	May 1998–July 1999		1 October 1999–30 September 2000	
	Number	Percent	Number	Percent
India	63,900	47.5	124,697	48.4
China	12,400	9.2	22,570	8.8
United Kingdom	4,400	3.3	7,937	3.1
Canada	4,000	3.0	8,365	3.2
Philippines	3,700	2.8	7,396	2.9
Korea	3,100	2.3	4,815	1.9
Taiwan	2,800	2.1	5,420	2.1
Japan	2,700	2.1	4,919	1.9
Other Countries	37,400	27.8	71,521	27.8
Total	134,400	100.0	257,640	100.0

Source: U.S. Immigration and Naturalization Service, *Leading Employers of Specialty Occupation Workers (H-1B): October 1999 to February 2000* (2000); *Report on the Characteristics of Specialty Occupation Workers (H-1B): May 1998 to July 1999* (2000).

TABLE 3

Occupational Characteristics of Specialty Workers (H1-B)

Labor Condition Application	Fiscal Year 2000		Fiscal Year 2001	
(LCA) Category and Code	Number	Percent	Number	Percent
Computer-related occupations (03)	148,426	57.1	191,397	58.2
Architecture, engineering, and surveying (00, 01)	31,384	12.1	40,388	12.3
Administrative specializations (16)	18,419	7.1	23,794	7.2
Education (09)	12,648	4.8	17,431	5.3
Managers and officials, not elsewhere classified (18)	12,423	4.8	10,065	3.1
Medicine and health (07)	7,781	3.0	11,334	3.4
Life sciences (04)	5,179	2.0	6,492	2.0
Social sciences (05)	5,010	1.9	6,145	1.9
Mathematics and physical sciences (02)	4,748	1.8	5,772	1.8
Miscellaneous professional, technical, and managerial (19)	4,276	1.6	5,662	1.7
Art (14)	3,046	1.2	3,425	1.0
Writing (13)	1,501	0.6	1,888	0.6
Law and jurisprudence (11)	1,132	0.4	1,614	0.5
Fashion models (29)	781	0.3	910	0.3
Entertainment and recreation (15)	727	0.3	772	0.2
Museum, library, and archival sciences (10)	330	0.1	336	0.1
Religion and theology (12)	103	0.0	83	0.0
Occupation unknown	2,084	0.8	1,340	0.4
Total	259,998	100.0	328,848	100.0

Source: U.S. Immigration and Naturalization Service, *Report on Characteristics of Specialty Occupation Workers (H-1B): Fiscal Year 2000* (2002), *Report on Characteristics of Specialty Occupation Workers (H-1B): Fiscal Year 2001* (2002).

TABLE 4

Field research: Companies Visited, 1999–2000

Company ID	Ownership	Year of Inception	Total Staff	Revenue in Rupees (in millions)	Revenue in U.S. Dollars (in millions)
C1	Indian	1997	45	5	0.1
C2	Indian	1990	45	9	0.2
C3	Indian	1996	25	10.4	0.2
C4	Indian	1968	11,495	16,900	368.6
C5	Foreign	1982	784	515.3	11.2
C6	Foreign	1997	492	60	1.3
C7	Foreign	1996	106	30	0.7
C8	Indian	1996	711	717.1	15.6
C9	Foreign	1998	2,366	4,515	98.5
C10	Indian	1995	61	75	1.6
C11	Indian	1994	8	5	0.1
C12	Indian	1995	25	30	0.7
C13	Foreign	1992	593	595.4	13.0
C14	Indian	1996	65	10	0.2
C15	Indian	1995	399	1,385	30.2
C16	Indian	1992	907	1,502.6	32.8
C17	Foreign	1995	30	10	0.2
C18	Indian	1995	10	n/a	n/a
C19	Indian	1997	32	50	1.1
C20	Foreign	1980	140	n/a	0.8

Notes

Chapter 1: Of Code and Capital

1. Coyotes are professional people smugglers who help migrants cross the border and avoid the Border Patrol, transporting them in trucks or vans to safe places in the United States where relatives or employers await them.

2. Mortality among migrants has increased since the intensification of border enforcement, with causes ranging from hypothermia to dehydration to heat stroke as border crossers are pushed to ever more remote regions by enforcement efforts (Cornelius 2001).

3. The term "body shopping," because of negative connotations, is avoided in formal conversation. The more widely accepted term among programmers is "consultancy." I retain the term "body shopping" because it captures the sense of bodily presence at the site of work.

4. Russell attempts to save the quasi-permanence of a thing amid the plurality of events through what he calls *causal line*, which is not to be understood as *causation*. He has an often-quoted remark on the notion of cause: "The law of causality, I believe, like much that passes muster among philosophers, is a relic of a bygone age, surviving, like the monarchy, only because it is erroneously supposed to do no harm" (Russell 1913).

Chapter 2: Programming Globalization

1. By encouraging the "local" they also assume the other side of the binary: the "global," which appears as their own location and allows them to perceive economies and communities as local.

2. The butterfly effect is the idea that a very small change applied to a chaotic system at a certain point in time changes the future of the entire system in a dramatic fashion. Something as small as a butterfly fluttering its wings now might influence the weather system on a global scale six months in the future.

3. The term "developing" is problematic because it hides a progressivist discourse, assuming a single, linear path of socio-economic evolution for all nations. Therefore I intend its usage to be in invisible quotation marks; I leave off the quotation marks for readability.

4. Cognitive enhancement has been a feature of military research for a number of years, and has included the development of pharmaceutical agents intended to increase the alertness of soldiers suffering from severe sleep deprivation.

5. Edward Davidson (1868), quoted in Prakash (1999).

6. The H-1B is a nonimmigrant classification used for a foreign worker who is employed in a specialty occupation temporarily for a maximum of six years. A specialty occupation requires theoretical or practical application of a body of specialized knowledge, along with at least a bachelor's degree or its equivalent.

Chapter 3: Body Shopping

1. In the United States the "Green Card" stands for permanent residency.

2. The number of visas granted as a percentage of the population of the country of origin is perhaps higher for some smaller countries such as Hungary or Ireland, but I am more interested in the absolute number of immigrant bodies present in the United States, because a large pool of programmers eventually attracts more business to India through virtual methods as well.

3. I am using the term "universality" in the sense "the quality or character extending to . . . (more usually) a great variety of subjects" rather than "extending to all without exception." See *Oxford English Dictionary*, s.v. "universality," sense 4.

4. In my small sample of twenty-seven responses on the question of salary, the mean annual salary was $75,000, including both programmers and systems analysts with degrees from India and the United States.

5. The names and identifying characteristics of corporations have been removed throughout this book.

6. Habermas borrows the phenomenological notion of "lifeworld" (*Lebenswelt*) from Edmund Husserl and Alfred Schutz to signify the ever-present *horizon*, the taken-for-granted *background* of social action. Habermas seeks to free this notion from its ties with the philosophy of consciousness and associated problems by grounding it in language use, by representing it as the "culturally transmitted and linguistically organized stock of interpretive patterns" (Habermas 1988, 124).

7. For Habermas, if the processes of reproduction are disturbed, they will lead to a variety of crises.

Chapter 4: Virtual Migration

1. While *front-end* tasks refer to work completed by employees who enter information into the computer, for instance while sitting at the front desks (or front screens), back-end tasks refer to computer jobs behind the counter, or rather behind the screen. This difference can also be understood in terms of software users and software writers.

2. PING stands for Packet Internet Groper, a utility to determine whether a specific IP address is accessible. It works by sending a packet or datagram to the specified address and waiting for a reply. PING is often used to troubleshoot Internet connections.

3. The demands of the system on people's waking and sleeping hours are not always transna-

tional: we are all aware that janitors and many other workers need to work at night or early in the mornings.

Chapter 5: Action Scripts

1. Mark Weiser of the Computer Science Lab at Xerox PARC describes ubiquitous computing as the last of three waves of computing: mainframe (many people share one computer), personal computing (one person with one computer), and ubiquitous computing (many computers, mostly invisible to the user, serve each person). Placing the origins of ubiquitous computing in postmodernism, Weiser conceives of it as a system in which the number of nomadic devices exceeds the number of people. These nomadic devices interact with a large number of fixed devices embedded in the environment (Weiser 1996).

Chapter 6: Code as Money

1. M1 is money that can be spent immediately; it includes currency in circulation and the checkable deposits in depository institutions (banks and thrifts). M2 includes M1 as well as assets invested for the short term, including money-market accounts and money-market mutual funds. M3 includes both M1 and M2 and such big deposits as institutional money-market funds and agreements among banks.

2. Code tends to go through a series of transformations from higher-level to lower-level languages. Programmers write programs in a form called *source code*. The source code consists of instructions in a particular language, like C or FORTRAN. Computers can only execute instructions written in a low-level language called *machine language*, however, consisting mainly of symbols and specific words, each of which directly selects a particular operation for the physical machine to perform. To get from source code to machine language the programs must be transformed by a compiler. The compiler produces an intermediary form called *object code*. Object code is often the same as or similar to a computer's machine language. The final step in producing an executable program is to transform the object code into machine language, if it is not already in this form. This can be done by a number of types of programs, called assemblers, binders, linkers, and loaders. See the Webopedia: http://www.webopedia.com/TERM/O/object_code.html.

3. Once I watched a talk show on which a Hollywood actress narrated how a male police officer had let her go scot-free for a driving violation. Another example is from Bollywood: the female star Deepika Chikhalia, who played Sita on a teleserial from the 1980s, "Ramayana," was let off by a traffic cop in Bombay, since he thought she was really the wife of Lord Rama.

4. Gautam Raghavan, Meg Shear, Kevin Tsosie, and Deborah Yun (Class of 2004, STS, Stanford University).

5. A marked rise in outpatient treatment of depression between 1987 and 1997 in the United States is understood as having resulted from better care, affordable new medicines, vigorous

advertising campaigns, and destigmatization of the problem (Olfson, Marcus, Druss, Elinson, Tanielian, and Pincus 2002), but the larger question is whether the predisposition to depression flowers in a "deworlded" space of social interaction. A slow emptying-out of the social in day-to-day life is surely a difficult, if not impossible, area of research.

Chapter 7: Migrations

1. I hope it is clear that fault lines among the three are analytical and discursive, not empirical, because nationalist, capitalist, and state programs may at times combine to produce specific effects in social life. For example, both state officials and capitalists could be driven by nationalistic concerns while adopting certain policies.

2. I do acknowledge capital's well-documented historical ties with nationalist as well as racist institutions. Capital also relies on cultural identities for understanding and encouraging specific consumption practices. My intent is merely to point out how capitalism, as a profit-maximizing enterprise, prioritizes in principle the quality and price of labor and associated transaction costs, and uses nationalist or racist institutions generally toward economic ends.

3. The attempted cancellation of the contract with Enron was based on a variety of factors, including alleged kickbacks to politicians of the former government by Enron and its extremely high user charges for electricity.

4. The informant is referring to software professionals who come to the United States to work onsite.

5. Under Section 10A / 10B of the Income Tax Act, a ten-year income tax holiday is available to the units that began software production on or after 1 April 1981 in any free-trade zone, or on or after 1 April 1994 in any electronic hardware technology park or software technology park, or on or after 1 April 2001 in any special economic zone. No deduction under this section will be available from the assessment year 2010–11 onward.

Bibliography

Abbate, Janet. 1999. *Inventing the Internet*. Cambridge: MIT Press.

Advertisement, Microsoft Office. 2004. *Wired*, March, 14.

AFL-CIO. 2001. "Recognizing Our Common Bonds." Web document, on file with author.

Alarcon, Rafael. 2000. "Skilled Immigrants and Cerebreros: Foreign-Born Engineers and Scientists in the High Technology Industry of Silicon Valley." *Immigration Research for a New Century: Multidisciplinary Perspectives*, ed. N. Foner, R. G. Rumbaut, and S. J. Gold. New York: Russell Sage Foundation.

Albrow, Martin. 1997. *The Global Age: State and Society beyond Modernity*. Stanford: Stanford University Press.

American Management Association. 1995. *AMA Survey on Downsizing and Assistance to Displaced Workers*. New York: American Management Association.

Anand, Utpala. 2001. "View from the Bench: Life, Laws and Liberty." *Silicon India*, May 2001, 46–52.

Anderson, Benedict. 1991. *Imagined Communities: Reflections on the Origin and Spread of Nationalism*. Rev. edn. New York: Verso.

Aneesh, A. 2001. "Skill Saturation: Rationalization and Post-industrial Work." *Theory and Society* 30, no. 3:363–96.

Appadurai, Arjun. 1990. "Disjunctures and Difference in the Global Economy." *Public Affairs* 2, no. 2:1–24.

Archey, William T., and Norman Matloff. 1998. "Should More Foreign High-Tech Workers Be Allowed into the United States?" *CQ Researcher*, 24 April, 377.

Aronowitz, Stanley, and William DiFazio. 1994. *The Jobless Future: Sci-tech and the Dogma of Work*. Minneapolis: University of Minnesota Press.

Arrighi, Giovanni. 1994. *The Long Twentieth Century: Money, Power, and the Origins of Our Times*. London: Verso.

Arrighi, Giovanni, Terence K. Hopkins, and Immanuel Maurice Wallerstein. 1989. *Antisystemic Movements*. New York: Verso.

Attewell, Paul. 1992. "Technology Diffusion and Organizational Learning: The Case of Business Computing." *Organization Science* 3, no. 1:1–19.

Balibar, Étienne, and Immanuel Wallerstein. 1991. *Race, Nation, Class: Ambiguous Identities*. New York: Verso.

Ballard, J. G. 1971. Interview. *Re/Search* 8, no. 9.

Baran, Paul. 1964. *On Distributed Communications: V. History, Alternative Approaches, and Comparisons*. Santa Monica: Rand Corporation.

Barnaby, Frank. 1981. "Social and Economic Reverberations of Military Research." *Impact of Science on Society* 31:73–83.

Baudrillard, Jean. 1983. *Simulations.* Trans. P. Foss, P. Patton, and P. Beitchman. New York: Semiotext[e].

BBC. 1999. "School Puts Spy Cameras in Toilets." BBC News Online: Education. 5 November. Web document, on file with author.

———. 2001. "Spy Camera Found in Toilet." BBC News Online: UK: England. 12 October. Web document, on file with author.

Bendix, Reinhard. 1960. *Max Weber: An Intellectual Portrait.* Berkeley: University of California Press.

Benjamin, R. I., D. W. Delong, and M. S. S. Morton. 1990. "Electronic Data Interchange: How Much Competitive Advantage?" *Long Range Planning* 23, no. 1:29–40.

Benjamin, R.I., J. F. Rockart, M. S. S. Morton, and J. Wyman. 1984. "Information Technology: A Strategic Opportunity." *Sloan Management Review* 25, no. 3:3–10.

Bhabha, Homi K. 1994. *The Location of Culture.* London: Routledge.

Bhagwati, Jagdish N. 2004. *In Defense of Globalization.* New York: Oxford University Press.

Bijker, Wiebe E., Thomas Parke Hughes, and T. J. Pinch. 1987. *The Social Construction of Technological Systems: New Directions in the Sociology and History of Technology.* Cambridge: MIT Press.

Bijker, Wiebe E., and John Law. 1992. *Shaping Technology, Building Society: Studies in Sociotechnical Change.* Cambridge: MIT Press.

Blau, Peter Michael. 1967. *The Dynamics of Bureaucracy: A Study of Interpersonal Relations in Two Government Agencies.* 2d edn. Chicago: University of Chicago Press.

Block, Fred L. 1990. *Postindustrial Possibilities: A Critique of Economic Discourse.* Berkeley: University of California Press.

Boggild, Henrik, and Anders Knutsson. 1999. "Shift Work, Risk Factors, and Cardiovascular Disease." *Scandinavian Journal of Work and Environmental Health* 25, no. 2:85–99.

Böröcz, József. 1997a. "Doors on the Bridge: The Border as Contingent Closure." Paper read at the annual meeting of the American Sociological Association, Toronto.

———. 1997b. "Stand Reconstructed: Contingent Closure and Institutional Change." *Sociological Theory* 15, no. 3:215–48.

Boyes-Watson, Carolyn. 1995. "Recordkeeping as a Technology of Power." *Berkeley Journal of Sociology* 39:1–32.

Boyett, Joseph H., and Henry P. Conn. 1991. *Workplace 2000: The Revolution Reshaping American Business.* New York: Dutton.

Brubaker, Rogers. 1996. *Nationalism Reframed: Nationhood and the National Question in the New Europe.* Cambridge: Cambridge University Press.

Buchanan, Pat. 2000. "Pat Buchanan on Immigration." Available at http://www.issues2000.org/Celeb/Pat_Buchanan_Immigration.htm.

Burawoy, M. 1976. "The Function and Reproduction of Migrant Labor: Comparative Material from Southern Africa and the United States." *American Journal of Sociology* 81:1050–87.

Bureau of Labor Statistics. 2000. *Occupational Outlook Handbook, 2000–2001.* Washington: U.S. Bureau of Labor Statistics.

Burnham, James. 1960. *The Managerial Revolution.* Bloomington: Indiana University Press.

Burris, B. H. 1993. *Technocracy at Work.* Albany: State University of New York Press.

Calavita, Kitty. 1996. "The New Politics of Immigration: 'Balanced-Budget Conservatism' and the Symbolism of Proposition 187." *Social Problems,* August, 284.

Calhoun, Craig J. 1997. *Nationalism.* Minneapolis: University of Minnesota Press.

Callaghan, Polly, and Heidi I. Hartmann. 1991. *Contingent Work: A Chart Book on Part-Time and Temporary Employment.* Washington: Economic Policy Institute.

Callon, Michel. 1999. "Actor-Network Theory: The Market Test." *Actor Network Theory and After,* ed. J. Law and J. Hassard. Oxford: Blackwell / Sociological Review.

Cao, Yu Uny. 1995. "National Committee on Immigration News Release." 12 December. Web document, on file with author.

Capelli, Peter. 1992. "Examining Managerial Displacement." *Academy of Management Journal* 35, no. 1:203–17.

Carrier, James G., and Daniel Miller. 1998. *Virtualism: A New Political Economy.* New York: Berg.

Castells, Manuel. 1975. "Immigrant Workers and Class Struggle in Advanced Capitalism: The Western Europe Experience." *Political Sociology* 5:33–66.

———. 1996. *The Rise of the Network Society.* Cambridge: Blackwell.

Cetina, Karin Knorr, and Urs Bruegger. 2002. "Global Microstructures: The Virtual Societies of Financial Markets." *American Journal of Sociology* 107, no. 4:905–52.

Chandler, Alfred Dupont. 1977. *The Visible Hand: The Managerial Revolution in American Business.* Cambridge: Belknap.

Chandler, Alfred Dupont, and Takashi Hikino. 1990. *Scale and Scope: The Dynamics of Industrial Capitalism.* Cambridge: Belknap.

Chase-Dunn, Christopher K. 1998 [1989]. *Global Formation: Structures of the World-Economy.* Lanham, Md.: Rowman and Littlefield.

Chattopadhyay, Basudeb. 2004. *A Jingle of Bells: A Short History of the General Post Office Kolkata.* Kolkata: K P Bagchi.

Clarke, Lee Ben. 1999. *Mission Improbable: Using Fantasy Documents to Tame Disaster.* Chicago: University of Chicago Press.

Clegg, Stewart. 1990. *Modern Organizations: Organization Studies in the Postmodern World.* Newbury Park, Calif.: Sage.

Clinton, Bill. 2000. "Remarks by the President." 26 June. Press release, Office of the Press Secretary, the White House.

Cockcroft, James D. 1986. *Outlaws in the Promised Land: Mexican Immigrant Workers and America's Future.* New York: Grove.

Cohen, Robin. 1997. *Global Diasporas: An Introduction.* Seattle: University of Washington Press.

Collins, H. M., and T. J. Pinch. 1993. *The Golem: What Everyone Should Know about Science.* Cambridge: Cambridge University Press.

————. 1998. *The Golem at Large: What You Should Know about Technology*. Cambridge: Cambridge University Press.

Constantine, Larry L. 2001. *The Peopleware Papers: Notes on the Human Side of Software*. Upper Saddle River, N.J.: Prentice Hall.

Cornelius, Wayne A. 1982. *America in the Era of Limits: Migrants, Nativists, and the Future of U.S.-Mexican Relations*. Working papers in U.S.-Mexican studies 3. La Jolla: Center for U.S-Mexican Studies, University of California, San Diego.

————. 2001. "Death at the Border: Efficacy and Unintended Consequences of U.S. Immigration Policy." *Population and Development Review* 27, no. 4:661–85.

Cornelius, Wayne A., Philip L. Martin, and James Frank Hollifield. 1994. *Controlling Immigration: A Global Perspective*. Stanford: Stanford University Press.

Cox, Kevin R., ed. 1997. *Spaces of Globalization: Reasserting the Power of the Local*. New York: Guilford.

Crozier, Michel. 1967. *The Bureaucratic Phenomenon*. Chicago: University of Chicago Press.

DARPA [Defense Advanced Research Projects Agency]. 2003. "Terrorist Information Awareness Program." *Information and Society*. Arlington, Va.: Defense Advanced Research Projects Agency.

————. 2004. "Combat Zones That See (CTS)." 25 March. Solicitation document, on file with author.

Davidson, Edward. 1868. *The Railways of India: With an Account of Their Rise, Progress, and Construction*. London: E. and F. N. Spon.

Davies, Glyn. 1994. *A History of Money: From Ancient Times to the Present Day*. Cardiff: University of Wales Press.

Davis, Martin. 2000. *The Universal Computer: The Road from Leibniz to Turing*. New York: W. W. Norton.

Dillingham, William P. 1911. *Reports of the Immigration Commission: Changes in Bodily Form of Descendents of Immigrants*. 61st Cong., 2d sess. Washington: U.S. Government Printing Office.

Doeringer, Peter B. 1991. *Turbulence in the American Workplace*. New York: Oxford University Press.

Dossani, Rafiq, and Ashish Kumar. 2005. "Weak Ties and Innovation among Indian and Chinese Engineers in Silicon Valley." Unpublished manuscript.

Douglas, Mary. 1978. *Purity and Danger: An Analysis of Concepts of Pollution and Taboo*. London: Routledge and Kegan Paul.

Drache, Daniel, and Robert Boyer. 1996. *States against Markets: The Limits of Globalization*. New York: Routledge.

Dreyfus, Hubert L. 1992. *What Computers Still Can't Do: A Critique of Artificial Reason*. Cambridge: MIT Press.

Dunn, Timothy J. 1996. *The Militarization of the U.S.-Mexico Border, 1978–1992: Low-Intensity Conflict Doctrine Comes Home*. Austin: CMAS Books.

Easwaran, Ashok. 2000. "US Handcuffs, Parades 40 Indian Programmers." *Economic Times*, 23 January.

Edmonston, Barry, and James P. Smith. 1997. *The New Americans: Economic, Demographic, and Fiscal Effects of Immigration.* Washington: National Academy Press.

Edwards, John. 2004. "Edwards Says It's Time to Outsource This Administration." 12 February. Press release, National Campaign Headquarters, Raleigh, N.C.

Edwards, Paul N. 1996. *The Closed World: Computers and the Politics of Discourse in Cold War America.* Cambridge: MIT Press.

Edwards, Richard. 1979. *Contested Terrain: The Transformation of the Workplace in the Twentieth Century.* New York: Basic Books.

Ehn, Pelle. 1988. *Work-Oriented Design of Computer Artifacts.* Stockholm: Arbetslivscentrum.

Espenshade, Thomas J. 1996. "Immigration in America's Future: Social Science Findings and the Policy Debate." *Population and Development Review,* December, 791.

Espenshade, Thomas J., and Charles A. Calhoun. 1992. *Public Opinion toward Illegal Immigration and Undocumented Migrants in Southern California.* Princeton: Princeton University Press.

Evans, Peter B. 1995. *Embedded Autonomy: States and Industrial Transformation.* Princeton: Princeton University Press.

Factories (Amendment) Bill. 2003. Government of India, 13th Lok Sabha.

Federation for American Immigration Reform. 2000. "Digital Addiction: Why the Information Technology Industry Doesn't Need More Temporary Foreign Workers." Available at http://www.fairus.org/html/digitaladdiction.pdf.

Ferguson, James G. 1999. *Expectations of Modernity: Myths and Meanings of Urban Life on the Zambian Copperbelt.* Berkeley: University of California Press.

———. 2002. "Of Mimicry and Membership: Africans and the 'New World Society.' " *Cultural Anthropology* 17, no. 4:551–69.

Foucault, Michel. 1979. *Discipline and Punish.* Trans. A. Sheridan. New York: Vintage.

———. 1991. "Governmentality." *The Foucault Effect,* ed. G. Burchell, C. Gordon, and P. Miller. Chicago: University of Chicago Press.

Friedberg, Rachel M., and Jennifer Hunt. 1995. "The Impact of Immigrants on Host Country Wages, Employment and Growth." *Journal of Economic Perspectives,* spring, 23.

Gage, Fred H. 2003. "Brain, Repair Yourself." *Scientific American* 289, no. 3:46–53.

Geiger, Theodor Julius. 1969. *Theodor Geiger on Social Order and Mass Society.* Ed. R. Mayntz. Trans. R. E. Peck. Chicago: University of Chicago Press.

Giddens, Anthony. 1990. *The Consequences of Modernity.* Stanford: Stanford University Press.

Gleckman, Howard. 1998. "High-Tech Talent: Don't Bolt the Golden Door." *Business Week,* 16 March, 30.

Granovetter, Mark. 1985. "Economic Action and Social Structure: The Problem of Embeddedness." *American Journal of Sociology* 91, no. 3:481–510.

Greenfield, Heather. 2000. "Guest Workers of the 21st Century." *TechWeek.* Available at http://www.techweek.com/articles/8-07-00/dc.htm.

Guillén, Mauro F. 2001. *The Limits of Convergence: Globalization and Organizational Change in Argentina, South Korea, and Spain.* Princeton: Princeton University Press.

Gupta, Akhil, and James Ferguson. 1997. *Culture, Power, Place: Explorations in Critical Anthropology*. Durham: Duke University Press.

Habermas, Jürgen. 1988. *The Theory of Communicative Action: Lifeworld and System: A Critique of Functionalist Reason*. Vol. 2. Boston: Beacon.

Haddock, Vicki. 2004. "Molester Multitudes: Police Can't Locate Thousands of Sex Offenders." *San Francisco Chronicle*, 21 March, § E, 3.

Hall, Stephen S. 2003. "The Quest for a Smart Pill." *Scientific American* 289, no. 3:54–65.

Hall, Stuart. 1996. "New Ethnicities." *Stuart Hall: Critical Dialogues in Cultural Studies*, ed. D. Morley and K. Chen. New York: Routledge. 441–49.

Handler, Richard. 1988. *Nationalism and the Politics of Culture in Quebec*. Madison: University of Wisconsin Press.

Hardt, Michael, and Antonio Negri. 2000. *Empire*. Cambridge: Harvard University Press.

Hart, P., and D. Estrin. 1991. "Inter-organization Networks, Computer Integration, and Shifts in Interdependence: The Case of the Semiconductor Industry." *ACM Transactions on Information Systems* 9, no. 4:370–98.

Harvey, David. 1989. *The Condition of Postmodernity: An Enquiry into the Origins of Cultural Change*. Cambridge: Blackwell.

Hawking, Stephen W. 1988. *A Brief History of Time: From the Big Bang to Black Holes*. New York: Bantam.

Heeks, Richard, S. Krishna, Brian Nicholson, and Sundeep Sahay. 2001. "Synching or Sinking: Global Software Outsourcing Relationships." *IEEE Software*, March–April.

Heydebrand, W. V. 1989. "New Organizational Forms." *Work and Occupations* 16, no. 3:323–57.

Higham, John. 1988 [1955]. *Strangers in the Land: Patterns of American Nativism, 1860–1925*. New Brunswick: Rutgers University Press.

Hirschhorn, Larry. 1984. *Beyond Mechanization: Work and Technology in a Postindustrial Age*. Cambridge: MIT Press.

Hirst, Paul Q., and Graham Thompson. 1992. "The Problem of 'Globalization': International Economic Relations, National Economic Management and the Formation of Trading Blocks." *Economy and Society* 21, no. 4:357–96.

———. 1996. *Globalization in Question: The International Economy and the Possibilities of Governance*. Cambridge: Polity.

"The Hitchhiker's Guide to Cybernomics." 1996. *Economist: A Survey of the World Economy*, 28 September, 3–46.

Hobsbawm, E. J. 1992. *Nations and Nationalism since 1780: Programme, Myth, Reality*. Cambridge: Cambridge University Press.

Hodson, R. 1985. "Working in High-Tech: Research Issues and Opportunities for the Industrial Sociologist." *Sociological Quarterly* 26, no. 3:351–64.

IFG. 2001. History of the International Forum on Globalization. Web document, on file with author.

Immigration and Naturalization Service. 2000a. *Leading Employers of Specialty Occupation Workers (H-1B): October 1999 to February 2000*. Washington: Immigration and Naturalization Service.

———. 2000b. *Report on the Characteristics of Specialty Occupation Workers (H-1B): May 1998 to July 1999.* Washington: Immigration and Naturalization Service.

———. 2002a. *Report on Characteristics of Specialty Occupation Workers (H-1B): Fiscal Year 2000.* Washington: Immigration and Naturalization Service.

———. 2002b. *Report on Characteristics of Specialty Occupation Workers (H-1B): Fiscal Year 2001.* Washington: Immigration and Naturalization Service.

"Indian IT Pros Cool to German Card." 2000. *Deccan Chronicle*, 6 September.

Johnston, R. J. 1982. *Geography and the State: An Essay in Political Geography.* New York: St. Martin's.

Kale, Madhavi. 1998. *Fragments of Empire: Capital, Slavery, and Indian Indentured Labor Migration in the British Caribbean.* Philadelphia: University of Pennsylvania Press.

Kanter, Rosabeth Moss. 1989. *When Giants Learn to Dance: Mastering the Challenge of Strategy, Management, and Careers in the 1990s.* New York: Simon and Schuster.

———. 1991. "The Future of Bureaucracy and Hierarchy in Organizational Theory." *Social Theory for a Changing Society*, ed. P. Bourdieu and J. Coleman. Boulder: Westview.

———. 1996. "Can Giants Dance in Cyberspace? Large Companies and the Internet." *Forbes ASAP*, 2 December, 247–48.

Keen, Peter G. W. 1986. *Competing in Time: Using Telecommunications for Competitive Advantage.* Cambridge: Ballinger.

Kerr, Ian J. 1995. *Building the Railways of the Raj, 1850–1900.* Delhi: Oxford University Press.

Kuhn, Thomas S. 1962. *The Structure of Scientific Revolutions.* Chicago: University of Chicago Press.

Kumar, Amitava. 2000. *Passport Photos.* Berkeley: University of California Press.

Kumar, Nidhi, and Nidhi Verghese. 2004. "Money for Nothing and Calls for Free." Corp-Watch. 17 February. Web document, on file with author.

Kunda, Gideon. 1992. *Engineering Culture: Control and Commitment in a High-Tech Corporation.* Philadelphia: Temple University Press.

Kurian, George Thomas, and Joseph P. Harahan. 1998. *A Historical Guide to the U.S. Government.* New York: Oxford University Press.

Lakoff, George, and Mark Johnson. 1980. *Metaphors We Live by.* Chicago: University of Chicago Press.

Latham, Robert. 2000. "Social Sovereignty." *Theory, Culture and Society* 17, no. 4:1–18.

Latour, Bruno. 1994. "On Technical Mediation: Philosophy, Sociology, Genealogy." *Common Knowledge* 3, no. 2:29–64.

Leonard, Karen Isaksen. 1992. *Making Ethnic Choices: California's Punjabi Mexian Americans.* Philadelphia: Temple University Press.

Lessig, Lawrence. 1999. *Code and Other Laws of Cyberspace.* New York: Basic Books.

———. 2001. *The Future of Ideas: The Fate of the Commons in a Connected World.* New York: Random House.

Leyshon, Andrew, and N. J. Thrift. 1997. *Money/Space: Geographies of Monetary Transformation.* London: Routledge.

MacKenzie, Donald. 2003. "An Equation and Its Worlds: *Bricolage*, Exemplars, Disunity and Performativity in Financial Economics." Paper read at the conference Inside Financial Markets: Knowledge and Interaction Patterns in Global Markets, 15–18 May, Konstanz.

MacKenzie, Donald A., and Judy Wajcman. 1999. *The Social Shaping of Technology*. Buckingham: Open University Press.

MacPhee, Craig R., and M. K. Hassan. 1990. "Some Economic Determinants of Third World Professional Immigration to the United States: 1972–87." *World Development*, August, 1111.

Malkki, Liisa H. 1995. *Purity and Exile: Violence, Memory, and National Cosmology among Hutu Refugees in Tanzania*. Chicago: University of Chicago Press.

"Management Layoffs Won't Quit." 1985. *Fortune*, 28 October, 46–49.

Mantel, Hilary. 2000. *Fludd*. New York: Henry Holt.

March, James G., and Herbert Alexander Simon. 1958. *Organizations*. New York: John Wiley and Sons.

Marshall, T. H. 1977. *Class, Citizenship, and Social Development*. Chicago: University of Chicago Press.

Marx, Karl. 1998 [1887]. *Capital: A Critique of Political Economy*. Vol. 1. London: ElecBook.

Marx, Karl, and Friedrich Engels. 1985 [1848]. *The Communist Manifesto*. Trans. A. J. P. Taylor. London: Penguin.

Matloff, Norman. 1995. "Debugging Immigration: Immigrants with Computer Skills versus the Domestic Labor Pool." *National Review*, 9 October, 28.

———. 1996. "How Immigration Harms Minorities." *Public Interest*, summer, 61.

McConnell, Sheila. 1996. "The Role of Computers in Reshaping the Workplace." *Monthly Labor Review*, August, 3–5.

McCullough, Malcolm. 1996. *Abstracting Craft: The Practiced Digital Hand*. Cambridge: MIT Press.

McKinsey and Company. 2003. "Offshoring: Is It a Win-Win Game?" San Francisco: McKinsey Global Institute.

McLuhan, Marshall. 1994 [1964]. *Understanding Media: The Extensions of Man*. Cambridge: MIT Press.

Melbin, Murray. 1987. *Night as Frontier: Colonizing the World after Dark*. New York: Free Press.

Merton, Robert King. 1949. *Social Theory and Social Structure*. Glencoe, Ill.: Free Press.

Meyer, John W. 1980. "The World Polity and the Authority of the Nation-State." *Studies in Social Discontinuity*, ed. A. Bergesen. New York: Academic Press.

———. 2000. "Globalization: Sources and Effects on National States and Societies." *International Sociology* 15, no. 2:233–48.

Meyer, N. Dean, and Mary E. Boone. 1987. *The Information Edge*. New York: McGraw-Hill.

Mills, C. Wright. 1951. *White Collar: The American Middle Classes*. New York: Oxford University Press.

Mills, Mike. 1995. "Gates Assails Bid to Curb Immigration: Microsoft Head Says Legislation Too Harsh." *Washington Post*, § F, 1.

Ministry of Labour. 2002. *Second National Commission on Labour Report*. Delhi: Government of India.

Mitchell, William J. 1996. *City of Bits: Space, Place, and the Infobahn*. Cambridge: MIT Press.

Moschella, David. 1998. "Foreign IT Workers? The More the Merrier." *Computerworld*, 23 March, 38.

Myers, Helen. 1998. *Music of Hindu Trinidad: Songs from the India Diaspora*. Chicago: University of Chicago Press.

Nasscom. 2000. *The I.T. Software and Services Industry in India: Strategic Review*. New Delhi: National Association of Software and Service Companies.

———. 2004. *Nasscom's Handbook, Indian ITES-BPO Industry, 2004*. New Delhi: National Association of Software and Service Companies.

Negroponte, Nicholas. 1995. *Being Digital*. New York: Alfred A. Knopf.

Noyelle, T. 1987. *Beyond Industrial Dualism*. Boulder: Westview.

Ohmae, Kenichi. 1985. *Triad Power: The Coming Shape of Global Competition*. New York: Free Press.

———. 1999. *The Borderless World: Power and Strategy in the Interlinked Economy*. New York: Harper Business.

Olfson, Mark, Steven C. Marcus, Benjamin Druss, Lynn Elinson, Terri Tanielian, and Harold Alan Pincus. 2002. "National Trends in the Outpatient Treatment of Depression." *Journal of the American Medical Association* 287, no. 2:203–9.

Osterman, Paul. 1994. "How Common Is Workplace Transformation and Who Adopts It?" *Industrial and Labor Relations Review*, January, 173–88.

Parsons, Talcott. 1977. *Social Systems and the Evolution of Action Theory*. New York: Free Press.

Peano, Giuseppe. 1973. *Selected Works of Giuseppe Peano*. Trans. H. C. Kennedy. Toronto: University of Toronto Press.

Pedraza-Bailey, S. 1990. "Immigration Research: A Conceptual Map." *Social Science History* 14:43–67.

Pellow, David N., and Lisa Sun-Hee Park. 2002. *The Silicon Valley of Dreams: Environmental Injustice, Immigrant Workers, and the High-Tech Global Economy*. New York: New York University Press.

Piore, Michael J. 1996. Review of *The Handbook of Economic Sociology*. *Journal of Economic Literature* 34, no. 2:741–56.

Piore, Michael J., and Charles F. Sabel. 1984. *The Second Industrial Divide: Possibilities for Prosperity*. New York: Basic Books.

Polanyi, Karl. 1957. *The Great Transformation*. Boston: Beacon.

Porter, Michael E. 1990. *The Competitive Advantage of Nations*. New York: Free Press.

Portes, Alejandro. 1978. "Migration and Underdevelopment." *Political Sociology* 8:1–48.

———. 1997. "Immigration Theory for a New Century: Some Problems and Opportunities." *International Migration Review* 31, no. 4:799–826.

Portes, Alejandro, and József Böröcz. 1989. "Contemporary Immigration: Theoretical

Perspectives on Its Determinants and Modes of Incorporation." *International Migration Review* 23, no. 3:606–31.

Powell, Walter W. 1990. "Neither Market nor Hierarchy: Network Forms of Organization." *Research in Organizational Behaviour* 12:295–336.

Prakash, Gyan. 1999. *Another Reason: Science and the Imagination of Modern India*. Princeton: Princeton University Press.

Prasad, Monica. 1998. "International Capital on 'Silicon Plateau': Work and Control in India's Computer Industry." *Social Forces*, December, 429–52.

Prashad, Vijay. 2000. *The Karma of Brown Folk*. Minneapolis: University of Minnesota Press.

Presser, Harriet B. 2003. *Working in a 24/7 Economy: Challenges for American Families*. New York: Russell Sage Foundation.

Prince, Marcelo. 2004. "GPS Technology Helps Blind Find Way." *Wall Street Journal*, 17 March, § B, 4.

Prügl, Elisabeth. 1999. *The Global Construction of Gender: Home-Based Work in the Political Economy of the 20th Century*. New York: Columbia University Press.

Robertson, Roland. 1992. *Globalization: Social Theory and Global Culture*. London: Sage.

Ruggie, John Gerard. 1993. "Territoriality and Beyond: Problematizing Modernity in International Relations." *International Organization* 47, no. 1:139–74.

Russell, Bertrand. 1948. *Human Knowledge: Its Scope and Limits*. New York: Simon and Schuster.

Salzman, Harold, and Stephen R. Rosenthal. 1994. *Software by Design: Shaping Technology and the Workplace*. New York: Oxford University Press.

SAP. 2001. "MySap: Solutions for the New, New Economy." Web document, on file with author.

Sassen, Saskia. 1996. *Losing Control? Sovereignty in an Age of Globalization*. New York: Columbia University Press.

———. 1997. Immigration Policy in Global Economy. *SAIS Review* 17, no. 2:1–19.

———. 1998. *Globalization and Its Discontents: Essays on the New Mobility of People*. New York: New Press.

Saxenian, AnnaLee. 1999. *Silicon Valley's New Immigrant Entrepreneurs*. San Francisco: Public Policy Institute of California.

Schernhammer, Eva S., Francine Laden, Frank E. Speizer, Walter C. Willett, David J. Hunter, Irchiro Kawachi, and Graham A. Coldtiz. 2001. "Rotating Night Shifts and Risk of Breast Cancer in Women Participating in the Nurses' Health Study." *Journal of the National Cancer Institute* 93, no. 20:1563–68.

Schutz, Alfred. 1973. *The Structures of the Life-World*. Ed. T. Luckmann. Trans. R. M. Zaner and H. T. Engelhardt. Evanston: Northwestern University Press.

Scott, Alan, ed. 1997. *The Limits of Globalization: Cases and Arguments*. London: Routledge.

Selznick, Philip, ed. 1980. *TVA and the Grass Roots: A Study of Politics and Organization*. Berkeley: University of California Press.

Shaiken, Harley. 1986. *Work Transformed: Automation and Labor in the Computer Age.* Lexington, Mass.: Lexington Books.

Shannon, Claude Elwood, and Warren Weaver. 1963. *The Mathematical Theory of Communication.* Urbana: University of Illinois Press.

Simmel, Georg. 1990 [1978]. *The Philosophy of Money.* London: Routledge.

Simon, Herbert Alexander. 1997 [1947]. *Administrative Behavior: A Study of Decision-Making Processes in Administrative Organizations.* New York: Free Press.

Sindhu, A. R. 2003. Proposed Amendment to Factories Act. *People's Democracy,* 7 December.

Singh, Kavaljit. 1999. *The Globalisation of Finance: A Citizen's Guide.* London: Zed Books.

Sivanandan, Ambalavaner. 1982. *A Different Hunger: Writings on Black Resistance.* London: Pluto.

Sklair, Leslie. 1995. *Sociology of the Global System.* Baltimore: Johns Hopkins University Press.

———. 1998. "Globalization and the Corporations: The Case of the California Fortune Global 500." *International Journal of Urban and Regional Research,* June, 195.

———. 1999. "Competing Conceptions of Globalization." *Journal of World-Systems Research* 5:141–59.

———. 2001. *The Transnational Capitalist Class.* Oxford: Blackwell.

Slater, Joanna. 2004. "For India's Youth, New Money Fuels a Revolution." *Wall Street Journal,* 27 January, § A, 1.

Smith, Vicki. 1993. "Flexibility in Work and Employment: The Impact on Women." *Research in the Sociology of Organizations* 11:195–216.

Soros, George. 1998. *The Crisis of Global Capitalism: Open Society Endangered.* New York: Public Affairs.

Spufford, Peter. 1988. *Money and Its Use in Medieval Europe.* New York: Cambridge University Press.

Spybey, Tony. 1996. *Globalization and World Society.* Cambridge: Polity.

Sweeney, John J. 1999. "Making the Global Economy Work for Working Families: Beyond the WTO." 19 November. Speech before National Press Club, on file with author.

Turkle, Sherry. 1988. *The Second Self.* New York: Simon and Schuster.

Turner, Fred. Forthcoming. "Where the Counterculture Met the New Economy: Revisiting the WELL and the Origins of Virtual Community." *Technology and Culture.*

U.S. Congress. 1991. "Biological Rhythms: Implications for the Worker." Washington: Office of Technology Assessment.

Virilio, Paul. 1993. "The Third Interval: A Critical Transition." *Rethinking Technologies,* ed. V. A. Conley. Minneapolis: University of Minnesota Press.

Wallerstein, Immanuel. 1974. *The Modern World-System: Capitalist Agriculture and the Origin of the European World-Economy in the Sixteenth Century.* New York: Academic Press.

Weber, Max. 1978 [1921]. *Economy and Society: An Outline of Interpretive Sociology.* Berkeley: University of California Press.

————. 1992 [1930]. *The Protestant Ethic and the Spirit of Capitalism*. London: Routledge.

Weiser, Mark. 1996. "Nomadic Issues in Ubiquitous Computing." Web document, on file with author.

Weiss, Linda. 1998. *The Myth of the Powerless State*. Ithaca: Cornell University Press.

Wellman, B., J. Salaff, D. Dimitrova, L. Garton, M. Gulia, and C. Haythornthwaite. 1996. "Computer Networks as Social Networks: Collaborative Work, Telework, and Virtual Community." *Annual Review of Sociology* 22:213–38.

"White-Collar Layoffs Open 1990, and May Close It, Too." 1990. *Wall Street Journal*, 15 January, 1.

Whitehead, Alfred North, and Bertrand Russell. 1925. *Principia Mathematica*. Cambridge: Cambridge University Press.

Winner, Langdon. 1986. *The Whale and the Reactor: A Search for Limits in an Age of High Technology*. Chicago: University of Chicago Press.

Wittgenstein, Ludwig. 1922. *Tractatus logico-philosophicus*. New York: Harcourt Brace.

————. 1972 [1953]. *Philosophical Investigations*. New York: Macmillan.

World Trade Organization. 1999. Submission by the United States for the General Council for Trade in Services, WTO Work Program on Electronic Commerce.

Zaheer, A., and N. Venkatraman. 1994. "Determinants of Electronic Integration in the Insurance Industry: An Empirical Test." *Management Science* 40, no. 5:549–66.

Zelizer, Viviana. 1994. *The Social Meaning of Money*. New York: Basic Books.

Zerubavel, Eviatar. 1981. *Hidden Rhythms: Schedules and Calendars in Social Life*. Chicago: University of Chicago Press.

————. 1991. *The Fine Line: Making Distinctions in Everyday Life*. Chicago: University of Chicago Press.

Zlotnick, Hania. 1998. "International Migration, 1965–96: An Overview." *Population and Development Review*, September, 429.

Zuboff, Shoshana. 1988. *In the Age of the Smart Machine: The Future of Work and Power*. New York: Basic Books.

Index

157, 165–67; programming, 76; specific, 40; systems-level, 42; transnational, 1, 2, 5, 13, 59, 65, 89, 116, 152, 159, 169; universal, 40–41; virtual, 65. *See also* work

labor migration, 154. *See also* immigration

labor unions, 14, 15–17, 62–64, 163

local area network (LAN), 122

language: formal, 145; ordinary, 146

Latour, Bruno, 132

Leibniz, Gottfried Wilhelm, 142

Lessig, Lawrence, 8, 128

lifeworld, 91; colonization of, 47, 48, 50; system and, 47, 48, 49, 50, 51, 53

liquidity, 134, 135, 151

Luddites, 115

Marx, Karl, 18, 19, 67, 111, 135, 136

McCullough, Malcolm, 140

Mexican border, 29

Microsoft, 73, 75, 100–102, 115

middle managers, 102, 111–12, 125–26

Middleware, 121

migration, 1–16, 28, 30–35, 58, 63–126, 141, 151, 154, 157–69

mobility: material, 32, 33, 34, 83; virtual, 32, 33, 34, 83, 92, 162

money, 133–36, 149–51; liquidity of, 134, 135, 151; metallic, 133; modern, 13, 134, 135, 139

money of account, 150

Nasscom, 65–66, 71, 157, 159, 160, 166

national boundaries, 2, 11, 13, 27, 28, 152

nation-state, 9, 11, 18, 21–22, 26–29, 34, 61–62, 65, 73, 80, 141, 163; modern, 26, 29, 62

Negri, Antonio, 51

Negroponte, Nicholas, 32

network, 30, 31, 39, 68–69, 77, 84, 88, 111, 119, 120–26; distributed, 30; store-and-forward, 25, 121–22

network traffic, 122

New Delhi, 1, 33, 39, 44, 52, 70, 77, 79, 89, 91, 92, 167

Newton, Isaac, 6

Noida, 10, 74, 75, 89, 91, 160, 167

organizational structures, 13

outsourcing, 3, 16, 78, 161

packet switching, 121–22

panoptic governance, 12, 23, 103, 104–9, 127–29, 132

Parsons, Talcott, 135, 151

Peano, Giuseppe, 142

Peopleware, 101

Polanyi, Karl, 135

Portes, Alejandro, 38, 168

Powell, Walter, 126

power: nonnegotiability of, 146–48; relations of, 29, 106–11

Presser, Harriet, 8, 95

programming: eXtreme, 118; globalization and, 119; object-oriented, 118; online, 10; parallel, 83, 118, 122

programming languages, 5, 121, 130, 137, 138, 141, 144, 146

programming schemes, 23–26, 31–32, 34, 51, 67, 69–70, 77, 84, 93, 97, 99, 121, 129, 130–31, 146. *See also* algocratic governance; bureaucratic governance; panoptic governance

protocols, 25, 77, 84, 121, 124, 127; Internet, 25, 77, 121

rationality: formal, 104, 105, 106, 109, 110, 113; technical imperatives of, 105, 109

routing, 84, 120, 122

Ruggie, John, 18, 22

Russell, Bertrand, 7, 142, 143

Sassen, Saskia, 56, 64, 161

Schutz, Alfred, 81

Senate, 35, 153

A. Aneesh is an assistant professor of sociology at the
University of Wisconsin, Milwaukee.

Library of Congress Cataloging-in-Publication Data
Aneesh, A. (Aneesh)
Virtual migration : the programming of globalization / A. Aneesh.
p. cm.
Includes bibliographical references and index.
ISBN 0-8223-3681-2 (cloth : alk. paper)
ISBN 0-8223-3669-3 (pbk. : alk. paper)
1. Labor mobility. 2. Labor supply—Effect of technological innovations on.
3. Contracting out. 4. Globalization—Economic aspects. 5. Information technology—
Economic aspects. 6. International economic integration. I. Title.
HD5717.A54 2006
331.1—dc22   2005028238